PRAISE FOR THE BOOK

"David Gray's work is not just a handbook for the new generation of American Church leaders, he offers us a refreshing testimony to the way spiritual practice and flexibility can ensure the high wire act of balancing work inside and outside the home becomes—truly—a closer walk with God."
—Chloe Breyer, executive director, The Interfaith Center of New York; associate priest at St. Mary's Episcopal Church in New York; and author of *The Close*.

"I wish I had read this book when my children were young. David Gray tackles a fundamental 21st century challenge: how can workplaces provide needed flexibility so parents can mindfully and effectively meet the demands of work and family? *Practicing Balance* is a compelling, insightful, and joyous meditation on how parents and their employers can successfully address this challenge."
—Kathleen Christensen, Alfred P. Sloan Foundation, New York, New York

"Many people in the political world look at things as an either/or. There's often little room to explore common ground. But throughout his career in Washington, David Gray has opened our eyes to shared interests and circumstance. This book draws on Gray's life as a pastor, father, and policy-maker. It provides a road map to the critical work-life tensions so many of us struggle with and illuminates a meaningful path forward."
—Katie Corrigan, policy director, Kalmanovitz Initiative for Labor and the Working Poor, Georgetown University

"This book on religion and work-life needed to be written and must be read. David Gray offers profound redefinitions (the real balance is between activities that deplete versus enhance our energy), insightful questions for reflection, and extremely helpful advice about how religious practices can make us live calmer and more purposeful lives."
—Ellen Galinsky, president, Families and Work Institute and author of *Mind in the Making*

"Showing how religious communities can help lessen the work-family conflicts confronting families in an increasingly hurried world, David Gray breathes fresh air into a stale debate. *Practicing Balance* is must reading for anyone who cares about religion's role in supporting more humane and egalitarian options for time-squeezed men and women."
—Kathleen Gerson, professor of sociology, New York University and author of *The Unfinished Revolution: Coming of Age in a New Era of Gender, Work, and Family*

"For increasing communities of American culture, religious life is overwhelmed by secular busyness and complexity. Families hungry for faith are struggling to survive the flood. David Gray sees this silent tsunami and offers a lifeboat of ancient practice to carry church leaders forward to a faith filled habitable land."
—Gareth W. Icenogle, pastor, The West Side Presbyterian Church, Ridgewood, New Jersey

"Insightful writing by a pastor who understands from his own experiences of work, family, and religious life how important it is to embrace Christian practices of reading Scripture, loving family, and observing Sabbath. David Gray is a trustworthy guide to the balanced life, who walks beside us, not ahead of us."
—Douglas A. Learned, senior pastor, The Moorings Presbyterian Church, Naples, Florida

"I didn't expect John Calvin to provide the perfect mantra for work/life balance: "Rest, in order that God might work." This book by a practicing pastor in the capital of workaholic self-importance is a solid, practical resource to help clergy and their congregations find still waters and restore their souls."
—David McAllister-Wilson, president, Wesley Theological Seminary, Washington DC

Practicing Balance

Practicing Balance

How Congregations Can Support
Harmony in Work and Life

David Edman Gray

⊛ | ALBAN

The Alban Institute
Herndon, Virginia

The Alban Institute
2121 Cooperative Way, Suite 100
Herndon, VA 20171

Unless otherwise noted, all Scripture quotations are from the New Revised Standard Version of the Bible, copyright © 1989, Division of Christian Education of the National Council of the Churches of Christ in the United States of America, and are used by permission.

Library of Congress Cataloging-in-Publication Data
Gray, David E.
  Practicing balance : how congregations can support harmony in work and life / David E. Gray.
     p. cm.
  Includes bibliographical references (p. 125).
  ISBN 978-1-56699-430-9
  1. Time management--Religious aspects--Christianity. 2. Christian stewardship. 3. Work-life balance. 4. Quality of life. I. Title.
  BV4598.5.G73 2012
  248.8'8--dc23
                          2012023982

12   13   14   15   16   VG   5   4   3   2   1

Table of Contents

127889

Foreword

I was in awe sitting on the south lawn of the White House on September 13, 1993 watching the Handshake of Peace between Yitzhak Rabin and Yasser Arafat. As I looked around and wondered how I got there, for some reason I became very conscious of the fact that my hands smelled like peanut butter. Just a few minutes before sitting down with my husband to watch this historic event, I had packed lunches for our teenagers and sent them off to school.

It started as an ordinary day for our family, with the simple caring for our children, and we were then catapulted into that extraordinary moment. In hindsight I asked myself: Why was I experiencing that? What was the lesson of my thinking about making peanut butter sandwiches while history was being made? For me, it was a realization in the midst of a momentous occasion, that our caring for others—family, friends, community, country— is what life is really all about. Caring occurs at all levels and will, in the end, build the foundation for the harmony we seek in our world. Whatever our place and purpose, it is up to us to recognize and develop our God-given gifts and talents, and with a grateful heart, step out in faith each day.

When I was asked to write the foreword to David Gray's book, I was grateful to my friend for his faith in me and my mission. I have spent over twenty years in the work-life field and in the last ten have focused on community and family consciousness. From my experience, I have developed a mission statement to encompass my whole life: Using the gifts and talents given to me by God, I will dedicate my life to inspire, promote, and maintain a sense of family consciousness in my home, my workplace, and my community.

As a non-profit CEO and the spouse of a mayor, U.S. Senator, governor, and Cabinet secretary (celebrating thirty-five years of marriage this year), I have turned to this mission statement for guidance and strength in many situations. It has helped remind me that my work at home, in the marketplace, and in the community is connected to my faith. My path has been to pursue these ideals first at a local level and then on a national level with thought leaders like David Gray. I connected immediately with David because he too has sought to live out similar values. The way he has woven family, faith, and career together in his own life makes him well qualified to share the ideas in this book. David inspires us to advance the principles of a balanced life for our families, congregations, workplaces, communities, and nation.

He recognizes that balance is not a static state but a daily journey. David gives us not just the research and reasoning but practical tools and Scripture that emphasize the importance of the journey. Through his own experience in life, family, church, and government, David has explored the heart of spiritual practice and balanced living. It is a personal story for him.

In the pages that follow, David guides and gives rise to the changes needed in our thinking, our habits, and our society. He has beautifully outlined how in this book.

We must consider the national policies and societal influences that impact our ability to live a balanced life. Yet, if we are only looking outward to find balance and fulfillment in our professional and personal lives, we may forget to focus inward and care for ourselves. It is imperative as a parent, sibling, son or daughter, friend or neighbor, co-worker or boss that we find the strength to be gentle with ourselves so we can be there for others and meet our work responsibilities.

Self-care is important. It is part of our faith tradition. Too often we wait until we are not stressed and are organized to go to God for answers. Focusing on that relationship now can give us the strength to work it out. *Practicing Balance* is a resource that can help.

I am honored to be a part of a group of prayerful individuals that meets each week to read and to fulfill our need for in depth conversation about our faith. We come from different ethnic and religious backgrounds. We range in age from late forties to early nineties. Our group consists of a former educator and pastor's wife, a physical therapist, a realtor, retired clergy, a business executive, a grandmother and caregiver, and a non-profit CEO. We are a microcosm of family, congregation, and community looking for answers for our quality of life questions and spiritual understanding. In our search and sharing we recently read and discussed a book about Mary Magdalene. Focusing on her dedication to Jesus and her growth and understanding of his teachings helped us as we examined our challenges in loving God fully and loving our neighbors as ourselves while negotiating the 21st century expectations for work and life responsibilities. Mary's message to us was to remember that to love oneself and to love those around us is to love God. Our quest was how to exemplify this in our daily lives.

David's book more than addresses the answers we were seeking. It offers understanding, evidence-based research, and practical tools to help us all navigate our journeys. It encourages us to recognize our roles and opportunities to advance workplace flexibility. Its action plan encourages self-care that rejuvenates and restores. David provides a path toward work-life balance that can nourish us, support our families and communities, and allow us to be productive and creative in our work.

Whether it's the smell of peanut butter or something else, we all have triggers that remind us of our deeper selves and responsibilities. As you journey on your own path, I believe you'll find that this book helps you grow in life and in faith as it helped me.

Patricia Kempthorne
Boise, Idaho
July 2012

Preface

My dreaming has left me a treasure, a hope that is strong
and true,
From wasted hours I have built my life and found my faith
anew.

—Anonymous

This book is about a simple idea—that faith can lead to a more balanced life. It's about why Christians should take the problem of work-life imbalance seriously and about how we can use the resources of our faith to do something about this issue, both individually and collectively. While work-life imbalance is a national concern that does not receive the attention it should, it is a particularly critical challenge for American Christians because it gets in the way of spiritual development, church attendance, and member involvement. Work-life imbalance is an issue that deserves attention from congregational leaders.

What is work-life imbalance? You might answer that question by reflecting on your own life. Do you feel stretched and unsettled? Does it seem like you never have enough time to do everything you feel you need and want to do? Do you experience conflicts between your job and your family life? Do you feel you cannot get enough rest, volunteer at your church as often as you'd like, or devote enough time to your own physical, emotional, and spiritual well-being? Do you have trouble finding harmony between the things you must do and the things you would like to do? Do you rush from appointment to appointment, frequently multitasking? Do you feel as if your life is fragmented, leaving you with insufficient time to accomplish things that require a significant time investment? These feelings could well be symptoms of work-life imbalance.

If you answered yes to any of these questions, you are not alone. Millions of Americans feel they are rushing through life and experience competition between their work and non-work lives. Parents of young children often feel especially squeezed between work requirements and family obligations. Chances are your congregation is full of families that are experiencing such pressure; if not, chances are that you would *like* your congregation to be full of such people. Christian congregations of most denominations and traditions have been losing members in recent years and are experiencing "graying" trends as their memberships age. My own denomination, the Presbyterian Church USA (PCUSA), saw its membership decline by 3 percent during 2009, and the average age of members is sixty-one.[1] As leaders look to help their congregations grow, particularly by attracting families with children, we would do well to understand, account for, and offer resources that address work-life imbalance.

Moreover, congregations of all faith traditions are called to meet the needs of their communities and world and to help members deal with the problems they face. Beyond that, members of many faith traditions—from Muslims to Hindus to Jews to Christians—take seriously the call to care for our world by trying to improve it. As they seek to energize, educate, equip, console, and strengthen their members, U.S. congregations should care about and address the challenges and stresses their members face. The mission of many faith communities includes helping members deal with the anxieties of our culture in order to live more fruitful lives. Stress and imbalance can prevent us from developing a deeper connection with God and from enjoying life.

Christian congregations are called to live out the values of Jesus Christ by caring for the world that God created and loves. I believe that equipping the members of our congregations to respond to the issues of work-life imbalance is an important part of living out that calling. In addressing these concerns, I will draw on my own Reformed Christian tradition—in particular on the ideas of John Calvin, the sixteenth-century Protestant theologian whose writings helped shape the Presbyterian church. Calvin's ideas are important because they can contribute to work-life imbalance, yet they can also help religious Americans develop attitudes and practices that can lead to better balance. I believe the principles I explore in this book can benefit people from a variety of backgrounds, helping Christians discover the resources within our own faith that can lead to better balance, while also motivating people who are not Christian to seek answers within their own traditions to the challenges of work-life imbalance.

The relationship of work and family life in America has changed over the past few decades. Families are different today from what they were a generation or two ago. In 1970, almost two-thirds of married couples had one spouse at home full-time to handle the needs of the family. Today, more than 58 percent of married couples have both parents working outside the home. Many families must negotiate and juggle the demands of work and family in ways that were unknown to previous generations. School events compete with church activities. Many Americans whose children are no longer in the home are now trying to figure out how to take care of aging parents. Smartphones, laptop computers, and other mobile devices allow people to take their work with them wherever they go. These developments add to the imbalances between work and life experienced by many modern American families.

One reason Americans feel so stretched is that we have a complicated relationship with work. Work outside the home is important to most Americans. Most of us need to work a paid job to make a living. Work also provides a sense of purpose and meaning, because we find value in contributing to activities, organizations, and causes in the workplace. Work in the home is important too. The jobs we do raising children and caring for one another are vital. They are also not easy. They are also work.

The American Dream that "anyone can make it if they work hard enough" has spurred many people to invest themselves in their jobs. Many folks are working forty, fifty, sixty hours a week—or more. The typical U.S. worker today labors several hours more per week than the average worker a generation ago—and more than the average worker in most other developed countries. Many of us find that these long hours get in the way of our nurturing our relationships with children, spouses, friends, God, and self.

While many Americans are working harder than they would like, the Great Recession that began in 2008 has increased unemployment, leaving many others working less than they would like. Many of these people are looking for full-time work, while piecing together several part-time jobs to make ends meet.

These situations have personal, national, and religious implications. Many of us are harming our health through overwork. But each one of us who struggles with overwork and imbalance in life has an opportunity to make a change. We should take seriously the goal of living with balance. I take this issue personally. For much of my professional life I have either worked hard at my job, worked more than one job, or worked while also attending school. Along with my wife, who has also worked outside the home part of that time, I now share the responsibility of trying to raise four children. The biggest challenge I face in life is finding balance. My life as a pastor, researcher, husband, father, son, and citizen contains a mixture of joys, challenges, and sorrows, but at the center is the challenge of handling all these activities and still remaining balanced, healthy, and happy.

I write this book out of my personal experience as a parent and as a pastor who has the privilege of listening as people share their challenges with me. Increasingly, I hear about the work-life conflicts that people face. I have had dozens of conversations with people who have spoken about their struggles to find balance in life. As individuals with relationship, financial, and health issues have sat in my pastoral office and described their challenges, I have become increasingly convinced that work-life imbalance is at the heart of many of the physical, emotional, relational, and spiritual problems people face.

I believe work-life imbalance has become a national issue. Fortunately, the problem is gaining the attention of business and union leaders. Many companies and organizations are working on work-life balance solutions as a business strategy at both local and national levels. Moreover, the issue has caught the attention of policy makers in Washington. Numerous bills have been introduced in Congress to address the fundamental mismatch between the needs of U.S. workers and families and the structure of work in America. I had the privilege of being part of a group invited to the East Room of the White House when President Obama launched his Task Force on Middle Class Working Families, which included work-life balance as one of its priorities. This is only one of many national efforts underway seeking to enhance the flexibility of work in America for the benefit of families.

As I have read the social science research, listened to people's struggles, studied theology as a pastor, and dealt with my own work-life imbalance, I have come to believe that increasing workplace flexibility and deepening individual spiritual practice are two of the most important solutions that can help Americans—and particularly Christians in congregations—live a balanced life. Greater workplace flexibility can allow people to attend more realistically to both their employment and family lives. Enriched spiritual practices can keep people emotionally, spiritually, and physically healthy, so that they are able to meet their responsibilities and live life to the fullest.

My hope is that this book will help church leaders better understand the issue of work-life imbalance, realize its scope, and take seriously the role of faith communities in addressing it. I continue to struggle with living a balanced life. However, writing this work has helped me to reflect on and improve my satisfaction in life. It is my hope that you will make balance a priority, too, and that the resources of your faith can support you as you seek to balance the many activities of your life.

For Reflection

1. How rested, happy, content, and satisfied are you with how your life fits together?
2. What does *balance* mean to you?
3. Do you feel your life is in balance? Why or why not? In what ways is your life out of balance?

Acknowledgments

I'd like to thank all my colleagues in ministry for the motivation of their hard work on behalf of people who need support and for their attention to things of the spirit. I thank Beth, Lauren, Doug, Richard, and everyone at the Alban Institute for their skill and guidance; Lou and the faculty at Wesley Theological Seminary for their insights; Josh, Hafsa, and Kelleen for their research contributions; and the teams at the New America Foundation and throughout the Sloan network for their inspiration. Many thanks to all my friends at Bradley Hills Presbyterian Church for their partnership in spiritual ministry and for their support. To Susan for her input. Thanks to Kathleen and the Alfred P. Sloan Foundation for their support of this project. Thanks to Katie and everyone at WF2010 for their partnership. To my parents for their input and help always. And much gratitude in so many ways to and for my life partner, Bridget, and for our kids who are the reason I care most about balance.

PART 1

The Problem of Work-Life Imbalance

Chapter 1

It's Personal

Humans are always on the go, always moving fast from one place to another. Maybe that's why they call the human race a race.

—Wally, *The Switch* (Miramax, 2010)

One Family, Two Parents, Three Jobs, Four Kids

Life passes like a flash of lighting
Whose blaze barely lasts long enough to see . . .
—Hermann Hesse, *Klingsor's Last Summer*
(Farrar, Straus, and Giroux, 1970)

My first real job was working in a metals testing lab. My task was to place newly produced steel bars and tubes in solutions with bright, fluorescent dye and then hold them under an incandescent light. The point was to see if there were structural weaknesses in the steel. The dye would get into any cracks in the steel and the light would highlight those cracks and, thus, any weaknesses. We tested random samples from each batch to make sure they were sound before the orders were shipped out to the customers. For several hours each day, my task was the same—to put steel bars and tubes in the dye solution, put the samples under the light, and record the results. The job was straightforward and predictable. I looked around at my coworkers and saw many people who had been doing this work for years. The job did not have a lot of flexibility. However, the workday always ended at 5:00 p.m., and my evenings were my own.

In recent years, my work has afforded me more flexibility but longer hours. In fact, too often I have used that flexibility to add work in the evenings. I would work hard during the day and then come home for dinner. After dinner, I often returned to church for meetings, then came home to help put my older son to bed. After my wife and children were in bed, I often went back to the computer and worked for a few more hours.

There is an old Jewish tale in which a wise man sees a boy running in the street and asks him, "Why do you run?" The boy replies, "I am running after my good fortune." The wise man tells him, "Silly boy, your good fortune has been trying to catch up to you, but you are running too fast." Many people today run through life, often sacrificing their health, families, and enjoyment. Nearly 40 percent of Americans suffer from serious stress, too often related to work. Even young people are not immune. In 2009, three high school students in Montgomery County, Maryland, were recognized for succeeding in getting perfect attendance awards in school. They had not been absent a day for thirteen years, from kindergarten through high school. This is a great accomplishment, but it comes at a cost. These young people reported feeling "great stress" as they faced growing pressure to be perfect. What do you see when you look at your own relationship with work and life?

Like many people, I find work overwhelming at times. After several years in government, I attended seminary, interned as a hospital chaplain, and studied to become a Presbyterian pastor. Shortly after I finished my chaplaincy, as I was preparing for ordination as a pastor, I found that the accumulation of work over several years had left me exhausted. I needed to be refreshed by the Holy Spirit; I also needed to make some substantive changes in how I spent my time. So I prayed and committed to learn to live a more balanced life. I began studying how others had made work and family fit together. For a while I made pretty good progress. Life felt in balance. But then the children arrived. First, my wife and I had one son. Then, two years later, a second. My time was no longer my own. I was responsible for others. My wife had started a business that meant she was also working outside the home, so I helped cover at home—changing diapers, trying to put the babies to bed, getting up for late-night feedings. Like many families with two working parents, we had three jobs—two outside the home and one inside caring for our children and household.

Just when we'd finally settled into a routine with the two children, we had another pregnancy. I will never forget the day when my wife and I went to the OB. The doctor doing the ultrasound looked at the screen and said, "I see one baby . . . and now I see another." I was standing behind the doctor, who said, "I wish I could see David's face right now." My wife and I were astounded. "What? Twins?" Four children under five! We couldn't believe it. Sometimes life's unexpected challenges are the best parts of life, though they can be challenges indeed. One family, two parents, three jobs, and four children. At this point, I knew I needed to get serious about work-life balance.

I began to think about flexible work arrangements and deepened spiritual practices. I began working at home more and designating certain physical places at home for work and other places for rest. I worked with my employers and my employees, and we figured out ways I could spread out work to create more balance. Workplace flexibility became a critical component of my life. Most significantly, I turned to my faith and began to learn about and develop spiritual practices that had sustained others during the craziness of their lives. Daily spiritual disciplines became very important to me.

I don't have a perfect life now. I certainly continue to have my own struggles with observing Sabbath, saying no to requests, and doing my spiritual disciplines every day. I am a work in progress. However, for me, spiritual principles and flexibility have enabled me to find more of the work-life balance I had been seeking. I am sleeping more and in better health. I am more productive in my work and more present with my wife and children. I have more energy and am more contented. I am grateful for balance.

For Reflection

1. Are there times when your life has felt more in balance than it does now? If so, what conditions made it so?
2. Do you know anyone who models a well-balanced life? If so, what can you learn from this person?

THE CHALLENGE OF
BALANCING WORK AND LIFE TODAY

Most people (men) pursue pleasure with such breathless haste that they hurry past it.
—Søren Kierkegaard, *Either/Or,* 1843

Mary is a partner at a law firm in Delaware. She and her husband have three children. They attend a church near their home. A life-long Catholic, Mary is a committed member of her parish. She has served as a Sunday school teacher and has been involved with many other congregational projects. However, Mary feels stressed. She has so much going on in her life that she has trouble finding time for it all. One Monday she had scheduled a meeting with an important client. When she got up that winter morning, she found her eight-year-old had come down with the flu. Her husband was out of town on work, so he could not watch the child. She didn't want to leave her sick child, but she also felt a responsibility to her client. So she got dressed, asked her fifteen-year-old to stay home from school that morning to watch the younger child, drove to work, conducted her meeting, and then returned home to take care of her son. She felt guilty about leaving the sick child at home, making her older child late for school, and not being fully focused on her work meeting.

Khalil is a college junior. He has become interested in religion after taking a religion course from a professor who used to be a monk. Khalil considers himself a "spiritual" person but does not regularly attend any local place of worship because he does not feel he has time. He feels very driven to do well in school. His parents are involved in their congregation and have instilled in Khalil a strong work ethic. He says he would like to have more balance in his life, but his focus on succeeding in school does not allow sufficient time for personal activities.

Greg is a retired teacher and a part-time gardener. He is a deacon at his Presbyterian church. Greg has two grown children who live nearby, one of whom has a child with special needs. Greg and his wife spend much of their time helping care for their grandchild so their daughter, a single mother, can go to work. Greg has a heart for sports and for volunteering and has trouble saying no when asked to volunteer for community projects or coach a youth soccer team. He was recently asked to stay on as a deacon for another three years and is reluctant to turn down the offer because he wants people to think highly of him. However, he has increasingly been feeling burned out. Greg's wife and daughter are starting to resent his activities, because they are getting in the way of his caring for his grandchild and being present for family and church activities.

Pam is a stay-at-home mom who is active in her local Methodist congregation. She'd worked for years as a registered nurse, but the job proved to be too much for her while she was also trying to care for two teenage children at home and assisting her aging parents who live nearby. Pam's husband works long hours as a policy analyst for the government, and her sister is going through a divorce. Her sister's personal situation meant that when Pam's parents needed to move into a nursing home, Pam had to manage the transition by herself.

Debbie attends synagogue most Friday nights. During the past several years, she has been asked to serve on several different synagogue committees. Debbie has declined each time because she does not feel she has time for such leadership activities. During the week she works hard as a financial analyst. She says the Friday evening worship service helps her feel grounded. On her Sabbath, Debbie feels contented. However, Sunday through Friday, Debbie does not feel connected to her faith. Rather, her life is stressful and out of balance.

John is a fireman. He has two children under the age of three and a wife who works long hours running a retail store. He attends a nondenominational Christian church. John is enrolled in a graduate program and volunteers for several community service activities in his area. John is often at home during the days while his wife is at work, and vice versa. This allows the couple to care for their children but creates a challenge from them because they are not spending enough time together. John and his spouse both lack "downtime" for themselves as well. When all their time is focused on work or child care, personal time is sacrificed.

For Reflection

1. Read Ecclesiastes 3:1-8. What does it mean to you that there is a "time for everything"?
2. If you could make one change to help balance your work-life obligations, what would it be?

HANGING BY A THREAD

*The trouble with the rat race is that even if you win, you're
still a rat.*

—Lily Tomlin, *People*, December 26, 1977

Nearly every one of us has struggled with work-life balance at
some point. For most of us, the issue is a very personal one. But
how do we define *balance*?

One consulting firm that works on these issues defines *balance*
as "Meaningful daily achievement and enjoyment in each of my
four life quadrants: Work, Family, Friends, and Self."[1] I think
that is helpful, but I've found that definitions will vary for individuals. In 2008, when I taught a seminar on the subject through
the Reformed Institute of Metropolitan Washington DC, participants shared many different definitions over the course of our
time together. But we agreed that a working definition of work-life
balance centered on a person's feeling satisfied overall with how
the various activites of his or her life fit together.

I have found that most people find it very difficult to achieve
complete balance between what they would like to be doing and
what they have to do. Who do you know who gets eight hours of
sleep, has a perfect job and family life, and feels totally at peace?
Who do you know whose life is in real equilibrium? Balance is not
a destination. It is a journey.

Work-life balance has, for the past generation, been an especially serious concern for many women in America. I know my
wife has been challenged by the issue. On the very day we found
out we were expecting our first child, she signed a lease on a store
for the new business she was opening. There was no getting around
the challenges she faced in starting a new business while beginning
a new family. Although we are both involved in caring for our children, we have no extended family living in our area to help. We've
tried all sorts of child-care arrangements, including bringing our

children to work meetings. We are well aware of what so many Americans also know: child care is important yet expensive.

For many women (as well as for many men), the desire for a family competes at some level with a desire and need for an income-producing job as well as the opportunity to pursue their interests and use all their gifts in meaningful ways. Women now comprise roughly half the U.S. workforce, but still bear the brunt of child rearing responsibilities and the majority of the housework in America. Women who have children earn less than women who do not. This underscores the challenge of work and family.

Over the past two generations, shifts in the prospects for and pressures on women have created work-life imbalances for many. According to *The Economist* magazine:

> The economic empowerment of women across the rich world is one of the most remarkable revolutions of the past 50 years. It is remarkable because of the extent of the change: millions of people who were once dependent on men have taken control of their own economic fates. . . . Many women—and indeed many men—feel that they are caught in an ever-tightening tangle of commitments. If the empowerment of women was one of the great changes of the past 50 years, dealing with its social consequences will be one of the great challenges of the next 50. . . .[2]

Although opportunities in education and employment have increased for women, these pursuits often clash with the pressure and desire to have and care for children and a household. As a result, work-family conflict is at the center of the agendas of most women's advocacy groups and is a concern of most of the working women with children that I know. It's why the White House Council on Women and Girls coordinated much of President Obama's work-family balance agenda.

Yet after a generation in which women's advocates have argued for attention to be paid to the work-life balance needs of women, at the March 2010 White House Forum on Workplace Flexibility,

President Obama argued that "Workplace flexibility is not just a women's issue."[3] I know from my own experience how personal the struggle to balance work and family can be for men as well.

A generation or two ago, most men were not greatly involved in child-care and house-care arrangements. Today, however, men are increasingly involved. Researchers from the Families and Work Institute found that as standards have changed and more men have become involved in raising children and in housework, more men now experience work-life conflict.[4] I know this to be the case. While I don't see my children during the day as much as I would like, I do sometimes come home for lunch or pick them up from school, and at the very least I try to be home in time to put my children to bed each night. Fitting it all in is difficult for me with evening meetings.

As men spend increased amounts of time with their families, the percentage of men who report experiencing work-family conflict has risen from 34 percent in 1977 to 49 percent in 2008—compared to 43 percent of women who report such conflict.[5] In dual-earner couples, 60 percent of fathers report experiencing "some or a lot of conflict today, up from 35 percent in 1977."[6] Ruth Davis Konigsberg's cover story, "Chore Wars," in *Time* on August 8, 2011, detailed the competition between men and women as now they both experience significant work and family conflict.[7]

According to *New York Times* reporter Tara Parker-Pope, "Several studies show that fathers are now struggling just as much—and sometimes even more—than mothers in trying to fulfill their responsibilities at home and in the office."[8] In 2010, the Center for Work & Family at Boston College released a study called "The New Dad: Exploring Fatherhood within a Career Context" suggesting that new fathers face a subtle bias in the workplace, because employers fail to recognize their stepped-up family responsibilities and presume that these men will be largely unaffected by children.[9] In the past, men were often focused on being the primary breadwinner in a family, but increasing numbers of men now report a desire to spend more time with their children. However, many lack workplace flexibility to enjoy that time. When it comes to taking time off for children, men often do not receive as much support as do women. The Boston College study found that when men need to take their offspring to the doctor or pick them up from child care, they often tend to do so in a "stealth" fashion rather than making a formal request for more flexible work arrangements.[10] It is as if many men do not want others to know they need support or help in balancing work and family.

In many ways, both men and women in many American families feel like they are hanging by a thread. Life is complex, like an interconnected web. We do the best we can to keep our stress within reasonable limits. Work-life balance is, in part, about keeping things under control, so the threads holding us don't break. If things don't happen as planned in one activity, everything might drop. If a parent gets sick, the whole family situation is affected, even collapses.[11] Men, women, and children are all impacted. It is a problem that needs attention.

For Reflection

1. Make a list of all the activities you are juggling today. Does it seem like you are doing more now than in past years?
2. Keep track of how you spend your time during the coming week, using the Time Reflection Chart in Appendix 1. This will help you consider whether you would like to make some changes in how you spend your time and, if so, how to go about it.

CHAPTER 2

It's National

If I had it to do over again, I'd have more of them [moments] . . . Instead of living so many years ahead each day.

—Don Herold, "I'd Pick More Daisies,"
Reader's Digest (October 1953)

A PROBLEM FOR AMERICA

Now I get me up to work, I pray the Lord I may not shirk. If I should die before the night, I pray the Lord my work's all right.

—A. Mortetta Fitch, *Brotherhood of Locomotive Engineers Journal* (1920), 859

You know the depth of the challenges that you and your family face balancing work and life. You struggle to get the food on the table each morning, get everyone out the door, and then arrive at the office on time with your presentation ready. You scurry to finish your work in time to pick up your children from school or practice when they need to be.

Now think of your friends. Are they facing similar challenges? When you take your daughter to a birthday party or watch your son's soccer game, do you find yourself talking with the other parents about "getting it all done," or the time squeeze they face, or how you are juggling all the activities in your life?

Now extrapolate for a moment. Are your friends and coworkers who share these issues unusual? I bet not. The reality is that millions of families and individuals face similar challenges.

Most of us enjoy the opportunity of work. Furthermore, we need the income. Yet too often the busyness of life dominates us. Our desire to do it all can leave us spread too thin—"Stretched," as Bilbo Baggins said in the movie *Lord of the Rings: The Fellowship of the Ring*, "like butter scraped over too much bread."[1] This is a central challenge for millions of Americans.

National statistics reveal the extent of work-life imbalance as an issue for U.S. families. In 2008, 42 percent of employees reported experiencing "some" or "a lot" of interference between work and family.[2] Moreover, in recent years:

- 76 percent of American mothers and 58 percent of fathers say they have "too little time for oneself."[3]
- 73 percent of mothers and 41 percent of fathers complain that they are multitasking "most of the time."[4]
- 69 percent of mothers and 68 percent of fathers say they have "too little time" with their spouse.[5]
- 53 percent of mothers and 37 percent of fathers report "always feeling rushed."[6]
- 52 percent of mothers and 58 percent of fathers express that they have "too little time" for their younget child.[7]

According to researcher Susan Bianchi, "Mothers did 22.6 hours of paid work per week on average in 2008, up from 18.8 in 1985."[8] During that same time span, mothers increased their time devoted to child care to 13.9 hours a week, up from 8.4 in 1985. However, they reduced their housework time from 20.4 to 17.4 hours and, according to time diaries, also reduced the time they devoted to self-grooming to 8.4 hours per week in 2008, down from 12.2 in 1985. As for fathers, they have increased their weekly hours on the job from 35.7 hours in 1985 to 39.5 hours in 2008. Yet fathers have also raised the amount of time they devote to child care by more than five more hours per week, now giving it 7.8 hours per week in contrast to 2.6 hours in 1985.[9]

As a result, most Americans have grown dissatisfied with their work-life balance. MSNBC has reported that 81 percent of U.S. workers are "unhappy with their work-life balance."[10] Many working parents are "sandwiched," caring for both young children and aging parents. The Families and Work Institute's Overwork in America study found that one in three American employees are chronically overworked.[11] According to the 2004 Attitudes in the American Workplace survey, 63 percent of Americans reported that job pressure interfered with family life, and 60 percent of Americans have reported feeling overworked.[12] Moreover, 63 percent of workers say they are stressed to the point of feeling "extremely fatigued or out of control."[13] Around two-thirds of both men and women report that they would like to work fewer hours; the percentage rises to three-quarters among those reporting moderate to high levels of work-life conflict.[14]

A 2006 survey by CareerBuilder.com sheds further light on the national problem of work-life imbalance, reporting that:[15]

- 33 percent of American workers report checking in with the office while on vacation.
- 50 percent of American workers report feeling a "great deal of stress" on the job.
- 37 percent of fathers say they would consider a lower paying job if it offered better work-and-family balance.
- 44 percent of mothers report bringing work home at least once a week.

- 19 percent of mothers report they "often or always" work on weekends.
- 36 percent of fathers say they bring work home at least once a week.

In addition, 17 percent of all employees have regular responsibilities caring for an elderly parent or relative and 42 percent have provided some elder care in recent years.[16]

So, if you think your life is out of balance, know that you are not alone. Work-life imbalance is a national problem. It affects most U.S. families. If your congregation is looking to understand, connect with, attract, and minister to families with children, it needs to appreciate the national scope of work-life imbalance.

For Reflection

1. Do you agree that work-life imbalance is a national problem? If so, what groups in America do you feel are most at risk?
2. Do you multitask? If so, in what ways does it help or hinder your work-life balance?

THE COSTS OF WORK-LIFE IMBALANCE

One stressed-out secretary told her boss, "When this rush is over, I'm going to have a nervous breakdown. I earned it, I deserve it, and nobody's going to take it from me."
—Billy Graham, *The Secret of Happiness*
(Thomas Nelson, 1997)

The stress of balancing work and family is taking a serious toll on businesses, workers, individuals, and relationships in the United States. The people in our pews are feeling it. Americans are just starting to understand the impact of stress on our work, our families, and our health.

Costs to Companies

Businesses experience significant problems when their employees have trouble balancing work and family. Such imbalance can increase conflict and employee turnover while decreasing morale and performance. When employees are worrying about whether their children are all right or whether they or their also-working spouse will get home in time to cook dinner, they are not as focused at work as they should be. Employers and employer advocates report that work-life imbalance too frequently leads to absenteeism and tardiness.[17] Stress and depression account for 200 million sick days a year in the United States and lead to the loss of nearly $105 billion in revenue.[18] The problem seems to be getting worse. An annual survey of unscheduled absences indicates that employee absences attributed to stress doubled from 1995 to 2005.[19] Significant health care costs for U.S. employers are due to preventable ailments related to lack of sleep, exercise, and poor diet.

The problem exists in other nations as well. According to Lisa Raitt, Canadian Minister of Labor, "The worst thing possible is for someone to get so unbalanced that they have to go on long-term disability or take sick days or go to work and just go through the motions. . . . It is one of the biggest issues we have out there in the workplace."[20]

William McNamara is said to have commented, "Perhaps the greatest malaise in our country is our neurotic compulsion to work." According to Luise Vassie, director of policy at the Great Britain-based Institution of Occupational Safety and Health (IOSH), "People are working harder than ever, but as our results show, too many are seeing their relationships outside of work suffer as a consequence. This isn't solely a problem for the employee—an unhappy worker is often an unproductive one."[21]

However, employees of companies that provide work-life balance benefits reported "fewer headaches and stress-related illnesses" and were 31 percent less likely to report lost productivity due to stress than were workers in companies that did not offer such support.[22] Employee respondents without work-life supports were 62 percent more likely to experience sleep issues that impacted their work and spent 20 percent more time dealing with dependent care issues on the job.[23]

Work-life imbalance is a serious issue for employee recruitment, retention, productivity, and success, and the costs of imbalance are significant. That's why some employers, such as Deloitte, IBM, 1-800-Contacts, and Johnson & Johnson, have worked to help their employees balance their lives, knowing it is good for business to have workers who are present and focused on the job.

Costs to Families

The costs of work-life imbalance for families are significant as well. According to the White House Council of Economic Advisors, the percentage of children with both or all their parents working full-time has increased from 25 percent in 1968 to 40 percent in 1988 to more than 48 percent in 2008.[24] More than two-thirds of American parents who work outside the home say they lack sufficient time with their children. These parents increasingly divide their time and attention among various activities. This fragmentation of life gets in the way of focusing attention on children. Working mothers on average multitask forty-eight hours per week while working fathers multitask on average thirty-nine hours per week.[25] Children notice the distractions and competing interests. According to a landmark study of children conducted by Ellen Galinsky, only 62 percent of children surveyed say their mothers can readily focus on them when they are together, and 52 percent say the same of their fathers.[26] Multitasking has the benefit of allowing working parents to spend time with children while still working. However, it can leave parents "frustrated, irritated, and stressed."[27] Roughly 45 percent of the children in another study reported that the time they have with their mother is rushed or distracted; 37 percent report this about time with their father. In light of these findings, it is not surprising that children don't necessarily wish for more time with their parents, but for their parents to be less stressed and tired during the time families do have together.[28]

The time crunch also forces many parents to neglect their own needs. Both mothers and fathers today spend less time on personal activities during their waking hours than did those of previous generations.[29] To ensure they spend time with their children, many parents end up sacrificing time they need for themselves, each other, and household functions. Researcher Susan Bianchi writes, "44 percent of employed mothers and 58 percent of employed fathers with a full-time employed spouse report insufficient time with children; 73 percent of mothers and 62 percent of fathers report insufficient time with spouse; and 74 percent of mothers and 58 percent of fathers report insufficient time for themselves."[30]

Moreover, parents can transfer a significant portion of the anger and anxiety they experience to their children when returning home from work. Studies show that the more we work and the more stressed we are, the more we transfer those negative emotions to our children.[31] Parents' stress can take a toll on their kids. Ask children how they are affected by their parents' stress. Children who say their parents are stressed out also say they feel that way. Some say it makes them feel sad, worried, or frustrated— feelings parents may not be aware of.[32] These dynamics can also take a toll on the children's schooling. Because rested, happy, and healthy parents are so important to the learning of children, when parents are stressed and do not spend sufficient time with their children, health and educational outcomes are impacted.

Costs to Health

There are national health costs to work-life imbalance.[33] Workers who experienced high levels of on-the-job stress are more likely to report poorer dietary habits, and many cite a lack of time for meal preparation as a reason for their poor diets.[34] Many families eat very quickly and often eat junk food. Nearly a third of U.S. children eat dinner with their parents three or fewer times a week. Less than 20 percent of families have dinner together consistently over the course of a week.[35] Lack of parental involvement in children's meals leads to unhealthy food choices. As families rush and eat more fast food, the high fat, sugar, and sodium content of such food can negatively affect the health of both children and adults. Over the past generation, as work and family conflict has increased substantially, the percentage of children who are overweight has roughly tripled. In 2008, 19.6 percent of children aged six to eleven and 18.1 percent of children aged twelve to nineteen were overweight.[36] Obesity has become such a serious problem in the United States that overall indicators of child health are now 30 percent lower than in the mid-1970s.[37]

Work-life conflicts among parents can also affect children negatively by getting in the way of doctor's visits, breastfeeding, and parental time to observe the health of children. According to one study, more than 40 percent of parents reported that their working conditions had negatively affected their children's health in ways that ranged from "a child missing a needed appointment with a doctor to a child failing to receive adequate early care which caused an illness or a medical condition to worsen."[38] Another study found that more than a third of children's behaviors could be explained by parents' work and stress characteristics."[39]

Work-family conflict also harms the health of parents. According to one study based on the National Comorbidity Survey, parents reporting stress due to the spillover of work to family life are roughly 2.5 times more likely to suffer from an anxiety disorder and twice as likely to suffer from a substance-dependence disorder than parents who do not report such stress.[40] In addition, parents reporting spillover in the other direction, from family to work life, were more likely to suffer a mood disorder and to have a substance-dependence disorder than parents who did not experience such spillover.[41]

Stress builds up over time. A British study that tracked the biological effects of work-related stress in a group of individuals for fourteen years found significant links to metabolic syndrome, a cluster of risk factors related to heart disease and diabetes.[42] Stress from work can lead to chronic hypertension and can contribute to coronary artery disease.[43]

Reports from the U.S. Department of Health and Human Services, including the National Institutes of Health, have found that many illnesses—both physical and mental—are linked to stress of some kind. According to Siri Agrell of Canada's *Globe and Mail:*

> Any time we're in a situation beyond our control, the brain releases two hormones, cortisol and adrenalin, which allow us to engage our fight-or-flight response. Without them, we would not recognize or react to danger. But when a brain is constantly stressed, confronted with a daily onslaught of overwhelming situations, it begins to pump out these hormones in excess, throwing off the body's other systems and overpowering the immune system . . . high levels of cortisol and adrenalin change the way the body stores fat, leading to higher rates of obesity, and increase its production of cholesterol and insulin, which cause heart disease and diabetes.[44]

Clearly, there are significant costs to work-life imbalance. It makes employees dissatisfied, it is bad for business, it undermines the development and relationships of children and adults, and it is bad for the health of Americans. As church leaders look to help people both inside and outside their congregations, work-life imbalance is an issue we should take seriously.

For Reflection

1. Do you sense any unhealthy work-life balance habits in your life? If so, what do you want to do about them?
2. Do you have any healthy work-life balance habits in your life? If so, write those down and reflect on them each day this week.

HOW DID WE GET INTO THIS SITUATION?

Busyness is the greatest evil to the spiritual life.
—Anonymous

In order to address the serious issue of work-life imbalance, church leaders need to understand how this problem developed and what is unique about this issue for Americans. The average American middle-class family increased its time on the job by eleven hours per week between 1979 and 2006.[45] On average, Americans work more hours than workers in most other nations.[46] The United Nations' International Labor Organization estimates that Americans work more hours than nearly any industrialized people and are increasing their work hours, while the trend in many nations such as France is to reduce work hours.[47]

Some researchers have compared individual Americans' attitudes toward work and our nation's public policies towards employment with those of European nations. I hosted an event once about whether the United States should try to be more like Europe. One person mentioned that one difference between the two populations is that "Americans live to work, while Europeans work to live." I'm told if you go to a dinner party in New York, people talk about what they do for a living. However, that is far less likely to be the topic of conversation in Paris.

Even those Americans who don't need to work so hard in order to keep the bills paid are increasingly choosing to do so. Sociologist Dalton Conley argued in 2008 that for the first time in U.S. history, higher-income Americans now work more hours than lower-wage earners.[48] It used to be in many areas that many lower income people worked especially hard because they had to. Now it seems that many people who do not need to work so hard for economic reasons are working harder than ever, driven not by financial need but by an ethic of trying to move even higher on the income scale.[49] Hard work and long hours have become badges of honor in some quarters.

Why do people work so hard in the United States today? There are many obvious answers. Many people love what they do and work long hours because they want to. Others don't like their job but work really hard because they need the money. This is particularly true in the wake of the Great Recession of 2008. Others work long hours in order to sustain the lifestyles they have chosen. We live in a materialistic culture, and we feel pressured to consume. Consequently, Americans have some of the lowest personal savings rates and some of the highest debt levels in the developed world, both individually and collectively. Americans are also influenced by a deeply rooted ethic of work. These factors, combined with the demographic changes of the past generation, have led to an increase in work in America.

Since its founding, the United States has attracted hard-working immigrants. Some hardworking Americans were brought against their will. Many factors that contributed to an ethic of hard work are rooted in U.S. history. But history has also seen attempts to limit worker hours throughout the world because of concerns about overwork. Around 890 CE, King Alfred the Great reputedly proclaimed, "Eight hours' work, eight hours' sleep, eight hours'

play make a just and healthy day," and in 1496 Henry VII reportedly ordered that the work day for field laborers should be capped
at fourteen hours.[50] In 1847, in the United States, women and
children gained a ten-hour working day; around 1900, the two-
day weekend started in many areas; and in 1926 Henry Ford shut
down his factories on the weekend saying, "The country is ready
for the five-day week."[51] In the early twentieth century, U.S. legislation began to protect employees. Child-labor laws, workplace
supports for workers, and improvements in working conditions
provided some positive changes for employees. When the Great
Depression hit in the 1930s, work became scarce in many quarters, and eventually the 1938 Fair Labor Standards Act (FLSA) was
passed. In an effort to spread jobs across a more widely dispersed
population, the FLSA instituted the forty-hour workweek. It speci-
fied that "blue-collar" or non-managerial employees who worked
more than forty hours in a given week would be entitled to be paid
"time and a half"—one and one-half times their regular hourly
rate. During the Depression, this law gave employers the incentive
to hire more workers; today, it continues to provide a significant
disincentive for some employers to require long hours. Overtime
pay does not apply to many "white collar," management, or service
jobs. However, since 1938, the forty-hour workweek has been a
restraint on overwork in America.

Domestic life and work-life balance in the West have been
greatly influenced by technology as well. Since World War II, auto-
matic washers, dryers, and dishwashers; faster cars and trains; tele-
phone advances; personal computers; and then the Internet have
led to an explosion of productivity for workers in industrialized
nations. It was thought in many quarters that these increases in
productivity would allow citizens to work much less. British Prime
Minister Winston Churchill foresaw "a time when accelerating
technological advancement would enable us to 'give the working
man what he's never had—four days' work and then three days'
fun.'"[52] If an employee were twice as productive, he or she might be

able to finish work by noon, it was thought, and have the afternoon for leisure. However, many Americans have chosen to work longer hours in order to earn more money. By and large we have been taking the post-World War II productivity gains in income rather than in increased personal time.[53]

Moreover, as noted, changes in the roles of women in the labor force and in society have had a tremendous impact on the relationship between families and work. Traditional gender roles in which men sought paid employment outside the home while women worked inside the home raising children continued for much of the twentieth century. The single income of the man of the house was sufficient to meet the complete financial needs of many families, while the woman took care of household needs. While this pattern was not absolute, as women have long been breadwinners in many families, this division of labor constituted what many have called the "traditional" American family.

Starting in the 1960s, however, a shift occurred as women entered and began staying in the paid workforce in greater numbers. In the forty years between 1965 and 2005, the percentage of two-parent, dual-earner families with children under the age of eighteen—households without a stay-at-home parent—doubled, from 28 percent in 1965 to 57 percent in 2005.[54] According to 2009 statistics, when single-parent families (mostly headed by women) where the adult is employed outside the home are included, the number of households without a stay-at-home parent is nearly 70 percent.[55] To put it another way, nearly seven of every ten U.S. families are headed either by a single parent who works or by two working parents. According to *The Shriver Report: A Woman's Nation Changes Everything*, women made up about 50 percent of the U.S. labor force in 2010.[56] The Great Recession of 2008 accelerated an increase in the relative percentage of women in the workforce (although the overall percentage of women in the workforce declined from 2008-2012), as the recession cut jobs in male-dominated industries such as construction, finance, and automotive manufacturing at a greater rate than in industries employing a higher percentage of women, such as education and health care.

During the 1960s, the desire of women to work and succeed in the workplace helped propel many into paid work. However, economic necessities have forced other women into the workforce. Since 1973, the costs of basic goods, particularly housing, education, and health care, have risen much faster than the overall inflation rate. At the same time, wages for most workers have not increased to keep pace. Many women wanted to work, but many also did so because their families needed two incomes.

Additionally, many U.S. families, particularly well-educated ones, are delaying having children. Delayed marriage and childbearing increase the likelihood that the greatest childrearing demands come at a time when job and career demands are also significant.[57] This can lead to further work-life conflict and stress.

Today, many families with children have parents who are both employed outside the home, often working a total of seventy or eighty hours a week at their paid jobs in addition to managing responsibilities at home. This means two people are struggling to handle three jobs: two paid-work jobs outside the home and one family-care job inside the home.[58] All these factors together mean the needs of families outstrip their resources, and work-life imbalance results.[59]

The demographic and social changes of the past few generations along with a lack of progress in other areas have helped lead to a national problem of work-life imbalance that negatively impacts U.S. businesses, workers, families, and the health of many. One additional factor underlies it all. For that, we turn in the next chapter to the impact of religion.

For Reflection

1. Do you find you work long hours? If so, why do you personally work as hard as you do?
2. Fill out or review your Time Reflection Chart. What does it tell you about how you live and spend your time?
3. Fill out and reflect upon the Tell Yourself about Your Time chart in Appendix 2.

CHAPTER 3

It's Religious

Certainly God is not a god in a hurry. That's clear. God is patient and subtle. God works through process and not through magic. . . . If God really is . . . the God of love, then that is how love will work.

—John Polkinghorne, mathematical physicist and
Anglican priest, interview with Krista Tippett,
On Being (National Public Radio, May 29, 2008)

Is there something deep in our DNA, history, culture, or economy that drives Americans to work hard? What role does religion play in the work-life imbalance of Americans? For one answer to this question, we now will consider the influence of Christianity.

In this chapter we'll look at how religion has contributed to the challenge of work-life imbalance and how faith communities are affected by it. Views that emerged from the Protestant Reformation, in particular the ideas of John Calvin, helped shape an ethic of work in early American settlements that has flowed through U.S. history and still matters today. In 2009, the world celebrated the five hundredth anniversary of John Calvin's birth. In March of that same year, *Time* included "the New Calvinism" as one of its "Ten Forces Shaping the World."[1] What is the substance and impact of Calvin's ideas and how have they continued to influence America's work ethic?

Religion is just one of many factors that shape Americans' desire and need to work. But as we look at the history of religious ideas—and particularly Reformed ideas—it is interesting to consider the ways in which religious thinking has contributed to the problem of work-life imbalance, as well as the ways in which church teachings can help address the concern.

Modern-day U.S. churches are affected by America's work ethic. As Americans devote more of their waking hours to work or family obligations outside the church, there is less time left for church volunteering. The results are fewer volunteer hours and more work piled onto the schedules of over-burdened clergy. Moreover, our pews are full of men and women yearning for help in dealing with the many difficulties stemming from their overwork at the office and home. Church leaders are often pulled in so many directions that they struggle to meet the demands on their own time, let alone help their congregations address their stewardship of time. Yet if the church is going to be relevant to its congregants, it must address this issue that is eating away at the spirits of too many religious individuals.

How Religion Has Contributed to the Problem of Work-Life Imbalance

Now we command you, beloved, in the name of our Lord Jesus Christ, to keep away from believers who are living in idleness and not according to the tradition that they received from us. For you yourselves know how you ought to imitate us; we were not idle when we were with you, and we did not eat anyone's bread without paying for it; but with toil and labor we worked night and day, so that we might not burden any of you. This was not because we do not have that right, but in order to give you an example to imitate. For even when we were with you, we gave you this command: Anyone unwilling to work should not eat. For we hear that some of you are living in idleness, mere busybodies, not doing any work. Now such persons we command and exhort in the Lord Jesus Christ to do their work quietly and to earn their own living.

—2 Thessalonians 3:6-12

In the Bible human work is at first presented negatively. Adam and Eve originally lived in the Garden of Eden in a state of bliss. They had plenty to eat, and while they were taking care of the garden, they didn't have to work hard. When they "fell" and ate the forbidden fruit, they were sentenced to hard labor. In heaven, according to many traditional visions, people return to an original blissful state of leisure.

Although some interpretations of Scripture consider work a punishment for sin, the views of sixteenth-century Reformer John Calvin, as understood by some of his followers, have contributed to a U.S. culture that reveres work. Calvin was a brilliant, serious, hardworking person. His mother died when he was four, and his father was the greatest influence in his life. Calvin struggled with his own vocation, in part because his father influenced him first to be a minister, then a lawyer, and then a minister again. At various times he worked as a minister, managed a church, reformed church law, preached almost daily, and wrote voluminously.[2] He studied with one of the best lawyers in France and wrote his masterpiece, *Institutes of the Christian Religion,* when he was only twenty-seven years old. Calvin even wrote many of the civil laws of the city of Geneva, Switzerland.

Despite doing many things well—or perhaps *because* he did many things well—Calvin worked on too many projects in too many areas to have real balance. This was the case even after he discovered that his primary focus should be on pastoring and interpreting Scripture. Calvin was aware that he worked too much and rested too little. He wrote:

Indeed, the fruit which my other attempts in the interpretation of Scripture have produced, and the hope which I entertain of the usefulness of this, please me so much that I desire to spend the remainder of my life in this kind of labor, as far as my continued and multiplied employments will allow me. For what may be expected from a man at leisure cannot be expected from me, who, in addition to the ordinary office of a pastor, has other duties, which hardly allow me the least relaxation.[3]

Theodore Beza, a French theologian who was a disciple and friend of John Calvin, commented that Calvin was frequently worn out. He didn't sleep much and often ate only one meal a day so he could continue to work. Because he worked so hard, he had stomach ailments. He lived to be fifty-four years old but his exhausting lifestyle no doubt contributed to his death in 1564.

Calvin believed contentment was important, however. Quoting 1 Timothy 6:6, Calvin wrote, "'There is great gain in godliness with contentment.' This may refer either to the disposition of our heart or to our actions."[4] Like many parents talking with their children, Calvin seemed to be urging readers to "do as I say, not as I do"—for he did not lead a balanced life. Yet the irony is that Calvin's very hard work has left Christians today with a copious body of wise and wonderful literature from him that can help guide our walks with God.

Some of Calvin's ideas contribute to work-life imbalance today because of the way some of Calvin's successors interpreted those writings. When Puritan Reformers in England came to America in the sixteenth and seventeenth centuries, they brought a brand of Calvinism that emphasized the importance of hard work.[5]

One well-known publication about Northern European heirs of Calvin and their attitudes toward work comes from the German sociologist and economist Max Weber. In his 1905 book *The Protestant Ethic and the Spirit of Capitalism,* Weber looked at the Western system of capitalism and argued that the value it places on hard work derived in no small part from its Protestant roots. In particular, Weber traced the Western work ethic to the ideas of Calvin. Weber started his analysis with the observation that more Protestants than non-Protestants were owners of capital, were in management, and were in the large business and trade enterprises of his day, and he wondered why.[6] He concluded that it was due to the influence of Calvinism, which had taken root in the late sixteenth and seventeenth centuries in regions of England and Holland and then was brought to America.[7]

The apostle Paul believed people should use the gifts God had given them rather than sitting on the sidelines of life. He warned the church at Thessalonica to avoid idleness (2 Thessalonians 3:6-18). Too many members of their community were so excited by the prospect of the second coming of Jesus that they abandoned their work to wait "in excited idleness for Christ to come."[8] Paul used the words *ataktos* and *ataktein*, meaning "to play truant," to describe the idleness of the Thessalonians, whom he viewed as truant from work.[9]

However, before Calvin, the most popular church view of labor matched the early pre-Pauline biblical depiction of work, largely holding that work was a "necessary evil . . . part of the never-ending, meaningless cycle of production and consumption."[10] To some, the important matters of life began once work ended. Many ancient Greeks believed the ultimate goal in life was for a people to reach a status where they did not need to work, although such a lifestyle often required a class of servants to do the work instead. In Thomas Aquinas's medieval worldview, work was only a necessary natural rationale for the preservation of life in a community.[11] Meister Eckhart, a fourteenth-century theologian and monk, suggested that an earthly focus on working hard to accumulate more material possessions does not contribute to a deepening relationship with God, writing, "If man is to be like God, to the extent that any creature may resemble him, the likeness will come through disinterest. . . . It is an achievement of the grace that allures man away from temporal things and purges him of the transitory. Keep this in mind: to be full of things is to be empty of God, while to be empty of things is to be full of God."[12]

Calvin helped change Western civilization's view of work through the concept of "calling." Before Calvin, Martin Luther, and other leaders of the Reformation era began writing about calling, the prevailing thought in the church was that God calls people to serve in the church but not in secular jobs—so only clergy were understood to have callings. However, Calvin, like Luther before him, emphasized the sacredness of ordinary vocations. Calvin believed all work had inherent dignity if given by God. He wrote:

> The Lord bids each one of us in all life's actions to look to his calling. For he knows with what great restlessness human nature flames, with what fickleness it is born hither and thither, how its ambition longs to embrace various things at once. Therefore, lest through our stupidity and rashness everything be turned topsy-turvy, he has appointed duties for every man in his particular way of life. And that no one may thoughtlessly transgress his limits, he has named these various kinds of livings "callings." Therefore, each individual has his own kind of living assigned to him by the Lord as a sort of sentry post so that he may not heedlessly wander about throughout life. . . . No task will be so sordid and base, provided you obey your calling in it.[13]

Calvin argued that God calls each person to a vocation and that the work of the laity can be sacred when done for the glory of God. Therefore, according to Calvin, one could act for God in any occupation—and this perspective elevated all work to a higher status.[14] Every job, every task, could have a certain dignity as a calling ordained by God. Calvin's views elevated business and industry and dignified secular work.[15] As a result, as David Hall puts it, "It is no accident that Rembrandt, Milton, Althusius, Grotius, Adam

Smith, and many others refined their callings while operating from a Calvinistic worldview."[16]

Calvin's view of predestination is also critical to an understanding of the Protestant ethic of work. In Calvin's view, God elects or destines ahead of time those who will live eternally with God.[17] Calvin wrote,

> Predestination we call the eternal decree of God, by which He has determined in Himself what would have to become of every individual of mankind. For they are not all created with a similar destiny; but eternal life is fore-ordained for some, and eternal damnation for others. Every man, therefore, being created for one or the other of these ends, we say he is predestined either to life or to death.[18]

The Calvinist doctrines, while perhaps sounding harsh to the postmodern ear, spoke directly to a question many in the Reformation-era church were asking: Are humans vessels of God's grace or simply worthless creatures condemned to the unending torment of hell?[19] According to Calvin scholar Donald McKim,

> For Calvin, the doctrine of predestination emerged out of a very practical situation. Why was it, he wondered, that some people believed in the Christian gospel and have faith, and others don't? That was a pastoral problem. Calvin's answer was that some people believed because God through the Holy Spirit granted them the gift of faith. This was God's election of these people to have faith, and thus to be Christians.[20]

Importantly, Calvin did not believe humans could know who is saved and who is not. Weber wrote that Calvin rejected the assumption that one can tell from the behavior of others whether they are elect or not, calling it a "presumptuous attempt to penetrate the mysteries of God." Rather, according to Weber, Calvin rejected this assumption suggesting, "In this life, the elect are indistinguishable from the reprobate for even the subjective experiences of the elect are possible for the reprobate too. . . . So the elect are and remain God's invisible church."[21] However, some of the Puritans who generally followed Calvin's teachings believed they could see signs of salvation from their work. That is, if a person found a "calling" in secular work and it proved successful, then perhaps that success was a sign God had favored that person.

Many Reformers who followed Calvin combined his doctrine of vocation or calling with his doctrine of predestination and began to look for answers to their urgent questions, "Am I one of the elect? How can I be certain of my election?"[22] Could hints of divine will for humans be revealed to the faithful? Many answered that it was possible to see evidence that a person was chosen by God. If a person worked hard, found fulfillment and enjoyment in work, and did well in his or her vocation, this success could be a sign that God had favored the person and that the person might be destined for salvation. Consequently, by being hardworking, meticulous, and disciplined in their vocations, Reformed Christians sought to prove to themselves and to those around them that they were worthy of membership in God's kingdom.[23] Hard work in a calling became the social product of a religious quest.[24] In the moral universe of capitalists that Weber was describing, work was no longer a meaningless chore. It was "invested with moral value."[25] Economic activity was seen as an end in itself, central to a person's identity, a calling with rigorous implications for salvation.[26]

Weber wrote that many Reformers believed, "God willed the social achievement of the Christians, because it was His will that the social structure of life should accord with His commands and be organized in such a way as to achieve this purpose."[27] Such thinking shaped early American religious leaders, including Puritan pastors and theologians like Matthew Henry, Richard Baxter, John Cotton, and John Bunyan. In their papers, books, and sermons, they were often critical of idleness and extolled the virtues of hard work. Puritan clergyman Matthew Henry wrote of the sinfulness of timewasting of all kinds, particularly through recreations, saying, "those that are prodigal of their time despise their own souls."[28] The prolific and influential Puritan theologian and minister Richard Baxter is the source of some of my favorite Reformation quotes about the importance of work. He wrote in his *Christian Directory*, "Work is the moral as well as the natural end of power. . . . It is the action that God is most served and honored by. . . ."[29] Baxter wrote, "Keep up a high esteem of time and be every day more careful that you lose none of your time, than you are that you lose none of your gold and silver. And if vain recreation, dressings, feasting, idle talk, unprofitable company, or sleep, be any of them temptations to rob you of any of your time, accordingly heighten your watchfulness."[30]

Baxter wrote further, "Outside of a well-marked calling the accomplishments of a man are only casual and irregular, and he spends more time in idleness than at work."[31] Baxter developed these points writing, "According to God's unambiguously revealed will, it is only action, not idleness and indulgence, that serves to increase [God's] glory. Wasting time is theretofore the first and most serious of all sins. The span of life is indefinitely short and precious and must be used to 'secure' one's own calling. Loss of time through socializing, idle talk, luxurious living, even more sleep than is required for health—six to eight hours at most—is morally, absolutely reprehensible."[32]

Although the Ten Commandments forbids worshiping idols, it would seem that for Baxter the great concern was not *idols* but being *idle*.[33] Baxter expressed the idea that every wasted hour means one less hour devoted to labor in the service of God's glory.[34]

In his seventheenth-century sermon, "Christian Calling," Puritan clergyman John Cotton spoke about vocation as a key part of God's plan for humanity. Cotton wrote, "A Christian may be busy in his calling from sun rising to sun setting . . . and may God's providence fill both his hand and head with business."[35] Cotton further wrote, "As soon as ever a man begins to look towards God and the ways of his grace, he will not rest till he finds out some warrantable calling and employment. . . . A Christian would no sooner have his sin pardoned than his estate to be settled in some good calling."[36]

These influential early American writers and preachers helped spread the Calvinist work ethic throughout the colonies. One individual in the pews was Benjamin Franklin's father, Josiah. A committed Calvinist, the elder Franklin passed on these teachings about the value of hard work to his son, Benjamin. While not as overtly religious as some other founding fathers, Benjamin Franklin translated these ideas into the secular language of the day through writings like *Poor Richard's Almanac*. Franklin's statements such as "time is money" and "early to bed, early to rise, makes a man healthy, wealthy, and wise," helped spread the Calvinist emphasis on hard work into the secular world in a way that influenced the development of the United States. Franklin even quoted, in his autobiography, the phrase from the Bible that his strict Calvinist father had drummed into him, "Seest thou a man diligent in his business? He shall stand before kings . . ." (Proverbs 22:29 KJV).

Alongside Franklin's secular ideas, the American ethic of work spread beyond the church through John Bunyan's *The Pilgrim's Progress*—a seventheenth-century allegory that, along with the Bible, was one of the most popular books in America for 200 years. Most Protestant homes had a copy of this tale focused on salvation, sacrifice, and the importance of hard work for the Christian. These ideas were passed on through literature and influenced writers, clergy, and leaders of the Industrial Revolution. Streams of immigrants brought their own ambition and were attracted to a nation that rewarded hard work. These factors, among others, came together to yield a culture that promotes work over the idleness Calvin feared.

Hard work leads to many good outcomes for people and nations. People in every culture work hard, either because economics require them to or because they want to. The Protestant "ethic" is not the only reason for the spirit of capitalism in America. Catholics, Buddhists, Jews, Muslims, and people of many other religious backgrounds—or no religious background—are also ambitious. The quest for personal satisfaction and economic factors like the need to support a family are among the many motivations that inspire Americans to work hard. Yet the influence of John Calvin has had a profound influence on the American ethic of hard work. Religion indeed has had something to do with the problem of work-life imbalance.

For Reflection

1. What do you think of this analysis of the impact of Calvinism on the work ethic of Americans?
2. Do you see a connection between your faith and how hard you work? If so, in what ways does your faith motivate you to work?
3. Fill out the Act and Evaluate Your Time chart in Appendix 3.

THE PARTICULAR PROBLEM FOR CONGREGATIONS

These people [pastors] tend to be driven by a sense of a
duty to God to answer every call for help from anybody,
and they are virtually called upon all the time, 24/7.
—Rae Jean Proeschold-Bell, quoted by Paul
Vitello in "Taking a Break from the Lord's
Work," *The New York Times*, August 1, 2010.

The Calvinist ethic of work influences members of today's Christian congregations. That obviously benefits the church in many ways. However, many congregations suffer from their members' and clergy work-life imbalances. Congregational leaders should recognize the serious spiritual impact of work-life imbalance. Because of the rise of dual-earner couples over the past generation; the advent of personal digital devices, smartphones, and other technologies that push work into the domain of the home; the impact of the recent recession on family income; and overwork in many sectors of society, work-life imbalance is an increasing problem. It is an issue even for high school and college students, who feel pressured to secure their futures by participating in an abundance of activities. Many such students have already developed patterns of imbalance that leave them feeling overwhelmed and will not serve them well as adults. Among church members, conflicting work schedules, a rise in the number of people who must work on Sundays, and the multitude of jobs and responsibilities now found within a single houseful often lead to conflicts with worship and other church activities.[37]

The church has both a responsibility and an opportunity to help. Our pews are full of stressed, overworked families who are harming their health and relationships with imbalance. Many come to worship and to adult-education classes looking for help with problems and questions they face. Most congregations talk annually about financial stewardship. However, very few congregations provide resources to help congregants deal with the stewardship of their time or assist them in coping with work-life imbalance from a faith perspective.

Many others in our local communities don't come to church at all because they don't believe they have time. School activities, sports practices and games, and work schedules all get in the way of church participation. Religious institutions should be places that teach productive approaches to work-life balance by providing resources that help their members, visitors, and those in the broader community become more like Christ. Such resources strengthen the body of Christ, help draw Christians closer to the model of their Lord, and provide an alternative to values—even religiously inspired Calvinist values—that are not serving people well. If we believe that work-life imbalance is a significant national problem and that Christians are called to make disciples everywhere, then churches should be involved in efforts to transform the world by countering problems like imbalance.

Work-life imbalance is also a major problem for clergy and other church leaders. The apostle Paul wrote to the church at Corinth about his strategy of "being all things to all people" (1 Corinthians 9:22). There is great merit to Paul's approach of meeting people where they are. Yet too often church leaders tire themselves out trying to be all things to all people. Stretched church budgets and increasing health care costs mean congregations are holding the line on increasing staff, even as congregational needs have increased. This has meant more demands on clergy, other paid staff, and volunteer lay leaders. Technology makes it harder to escape those demands, and the fallout for congregational staff members is significant. Lifeway Research has found that 65 percent of pastors work more than fifty hours a week and 8 percent more than seventy hours per week.[38] In particular, clergy work hours, stress, obesity, and burnout in mainline Protestant denominations are at an exceptionally high level.[39]

The compensation and personnel policies of my own denominational presbytery, the National Capital Presbytery, suggest, "For the health and well-being of both the pastor/educator and the congregation, attention shall be given to a proper work-life balance."[40] However, too many clergy are harming themselves because they lack proper balance. Paul Vitello reported in the *New York Times*, "Members of the clergy now suffer from obesity, hypertension, and depression at rates higher than most Americans. In the last decade, their use of antidepressants has risen, while their life expectancy has fallen. Many would change jobs if they could."[41] Rae Jean Proeschold-Bell, the leader of one study cited in Vitello's article, shares, "We had a pastor in our study group who hadn't taken a vacation in 18 years."[42] Vitello also comments that "cell phones and social media expose the clergy to new dimensions of stress."[43]

One reason clergy fail to achieve work-life balance is that many pastors have boundary issues and are overly focused on meeting other people's needs. Gwen Wagstrom Halaas, a family physician who is married to a Lutheran minister, has shone light on the issue of clergy health. In her book *The Right Road: Life Choices for Clergy*, Wagstrom Halaas suggests the problem is that many clergy believe that "taking care of themselves is selfish, and that serving God means never saying no."[44] Yet clergy are not Christ; they serve Christ. We all must rest, or imbalance results.

The United Methodist Church issued a 2006 statement encouraging their ministers to take all the vacation they were entitled to—a practice that is too infrequently followed in congregations of all denominations.[45] Episcopal, Baptist, and Lutheran denominations have all undertaken health initiatives that place special emphasis on the need for pastors to take vacations and observe their own "Sabbath days," with weekday time off in place of Sundays.[46]

Some Jewish leaders have expressed similar concerns about the need for balance among their own clergy. Rabbi Joel Meyers explains in his own context, "There is a deep concern about stress. Rabbis today are expected to be the C.E.O. of the congregation and the spiritual guide, and never be out of town if somebody dies. And reply instantly to every e-mail."[47] The issue is significant for Muslim clergy as well. "We have all of these problems, but imams are reluctant to express it because it will seem like a sign of weakness," said Imam Shamsi Ali, director of the Jamaica Muslim Center in Queens, NY. "Also, many mosques do not pay much and many [imams] work two jobs."[48]

Work-life imbalance is an issue not only for clergy, but also for other paid staff as well as congregational volunteers. Churches, particularly smaller ones, face volunteer shortages as many women, who have long composed the core of many church volunteer ranks, have entered the workforce in greater numbers over the past generation. Many mothers, who used to drive their children to church activities after school, now work until 6:00 or 7:00 p.m. or later. Churches struggle with attendance at after-school events because working parents are unable to bring their children, and churches compete against sports practices and games for the participation of youth on Sundays.

Kimberly Morgan and Sally Steenland write about this issue in a Center for American Progress report:

> Religious institutions benefited greatly from the traditional nuclear family, especially in the post-war years. Women served as volunteers, teaching Sunday school, organizing charity efforts, devotional classes, and more. . . . The concept of the nuclear family came crashing down in the 1960s. Divorce rates increased, women entered the workforce in record numbers, had fewer children, and challenged traditional gender norms. Women left the volunteer positions that had sustained religious institutions and led them to thrive.[49]

The crisis of clergy burnout and volunteer shortages results in part because the church has failed to model and encourage work-life balance. Yet, when congregations help their constituents with the work-life balance challenges of their lives, they can strengthen congregational morale, provide new opportunities for volunteers, and attract new members. One way congregations can demonstrate a better way to live is by giving their clergy, staff, and lay leaders the support and resources they need to balance their own lives. As congregations continue to develop and invest in resources of work-life balance, they can better model Christ's non-anxious presence and sense of balance to the world.

For Reflection

1. Does your congregation face volunteer shortages and time crunches among lay people? If so, what are you doing about it?

2. What resources does your congregation provide to help members and church leaders deal with the stewardship of time?
3. How should today's church (and particularly your congregation) support clergy and other church leaders in their work-life balance?

PART 2

Attitudes, Habits, and Policies that Encourage Work-Life Balance

CHAPTER 4

We Need to Change Our Thinking

The future is in God's hands, not yours. . . . Try only to
make use of each day; each day brings its own good and
evil, and sometimes what seems evil becomes good if we
leave it to God . . .
—François Fenelon (seventeenth-century cleric)

The first step in finding work-life balance is to change our thinking.
Our culture infuses us with deep and powerful values about the
importance of constant work and activity that can lead to imbalance. As we've seen, the beliefs of many Christians, particularly
those ideas rooted in the teachings of John Calvin, contribute to
the problem. Yet there are other Christian beliefs, including many
other teachings of Calvin, that can help us achieve better balance.
Changing our thinking and reconnecting to these values can make
the difference.

Although religion is part of the problem, it can be part of the
solution. The Hebrew word for "work," *avodah,* comes from the
same root as the word for "servant." If God calls congregational
leaders to lives of service following the example of Jesus Christ,

then seeking work-life balance does more than relieve our personal stress. It enables us to serve others as a way of honoring our relationship with God. I have found that the attitudes and actions of servanthood make me, and others I have worked with, feel more balanced. Moreover, when congregational leaders seek to honor God in this way, we can better understand the challenges faced by our congregants, particularly families with young children, and can guide our congregations to schedule programs at times that take into account the many demands on the time of church members. We can offer adult education classes on balance, and encourage our congregations to be more involved in changing national policies to promote balance.

Changing our thinking means developing attitudes to maintain a balance between using the gifts God has given us to work and care for children and family members on one hand and making space for activities and rest that help us rejuvenate on the other hand. I have found that my attitudes towards balance have been positively influenced by values and beliefs about four key concepts—stewardship, sanctification, self-care, and Sabbath—that have been shaped by my Reformed tradition.

John Calvin was concerned about idolatry—the tendency of humans to worship idols instead of God. Calvin believed God had revealed the severity of the sin of idolatry by making it the second of the Ten Commandments of the Hebrew Bible: "You shall not make for yourself an idol, whether in the form of anything that is in heaven above, or that is on the earth beneath, or that is in the water under the earth" (Exodus 20:4). Calvin confessed that he was guilty of idolatry and wrote about the idolatry of the images he saw within the churches of his day. Calvin believed people should be engaged in the world, but warned of the danger of worshiping the human use of God's gifts. Christians should worship God, Calvin urged, not human works.

The Oxford Dictionary of the Christian Church uses the Latin word *accidie* to describe "a state of restlessness and inability either to work or to pray."[1] Today, we use the word *sloth* (one of the seven deadly sins) to describe this state. Calvin was concerned about the tendency of some humans to ignore or waste God's gifts rather than following God's call to be involved in the world. When a friend asked Calvin if he would slow down and stop working so hard, Calvin responded, "What! Would you have the Lord find me idle when He comes?"[2] Given his concerns about both idolatry and idleness, it is ironic that Calvin married a woman named Idelette. John Calvin and Idelette de Bure Storder had no surviving children and their home life was marked by Calvin's very long working hours.

Between the two extremes of idolatry and idleness lies a balance. We should seek to use the gifts God has given us without worshiping those gifts or our use of them. That approach can lead to healthy balance in life.

As I've considered how my Christian heritage can support better balance, I have found four principles based on the four key theological concepts referenced earlier in this chapter, to be particularly valuable in seeking work-life balance: (1) Sometimes saying no is the right thing to do. (2) We should make rest a high priority. (3) We need to rethink what we mean by *balance*. (4) Living with balance requires that we be intentional about our use of time. We'll explore each of these ideas in this chapter. After we've thought about the ways our attitudes must change, the next step is to develop practices that can turn our mindset into healthy habits for living. In chapter 5, we'll explore how each of these attitudes can lead to specific habits or practices that can help us experience more balance in life.

SAYING NO

Our lives, in upheaval, have turned to a tizzy, never completing, because we're too busy.

All we must do for a tranquil soul, is to employ a word,
just one, called NO.
        —Anonymous, in J. Grant Howard, *Balancing
        Life's Demands: A New Perspective on Priorities*
        (Portland, OR: Multnomah Press, 1983), 144

To live a more balanced life, we must recognize our limits and
make choices. If we are going to find balance, we must set priorities—and that means saying no to some things. The theological
principle that underpins making such choices is called "stewardship." The Merriam-Webster online dictionary defines *stewardship* as "the conducting, supervising, or managing of something;
especially the careful and responsible management of something
entrusted to one's care."[3] For Christians, stewardship involves our
right management or use of what God has given us. Calvin wrote,
"Let this, then, be our method of showing good-will and kindness,
considering that, in regard to everything which God has bestowed
upon us, and by which we can aid our neighbor, we are his stewards, and are bound to give account of our stewardship."[4]

This concept of stewardship is rooted in Judaism, and
Christians can learn from the Jewish understanding. Jewish
scholar Joshua Stanton writes:

Stewardship is perhaps best understood in the Jewish intellec-
tual context as ideal human conduct—deeply and profoundly
ethical comportment designed to employ our human gifts to
the fullest. Conduct is the way in which we live our lives in all
respects, not merely those in which we feel particularly gifted.
More significantly, conduct or the way of behaving, is known
as Halacha in Hebrew—the same word used to denote rabbinic
law.[5] Through the application of and adherence to Halacha,
rabbinic Judaism suggests that a person may fulfill her ultimate
purpose as a sacred being, created in God's image (*b'tselem
Elohim*). It is, as the great philosopher-rabbi Moses Maimonides
explained, "God's way," and in an uncanny number of respects
parallels the ideals of Aristotelian Virtue Ethics. Through the

practice of virtuous behavior (as defined by rabbinic law), Jews may in time assume the attributes understood to be **virtues** within rabbinic thought.[6]

Congregations need to help members develop a concept of the stewardship of time as well as the stewardship of money. Financial stewardship campaigns or "calls for the offering" in worship services often emphasize the idea that everything ultimately belongs to God. Calvin wrote, "We are God's stewards of everything which God has conferred upon us."[7] He further wrote, "To acknowledge God's goodness with thanksgiving is the highest worship of God, to be preferred to all other practices."[8] God blesses us with material resources, but God also blesses us with time. We must steward our time wisely. We should begin each day with a word of thanks to God. Bruce Douglass of Georgetown University explains that one theme and common phrase of Puritan prayers was, "Thank you, God, for this day." Puritans gave thanks to God for the gift of time—a gift of God for each day.[9] Much as we recognize that all our financial resources come from God and "we can't take them with us," recognizing that our time is a gift from God helps us think seriously about how we use it.

Do we believe our lives belong to God? If so, how does that affect the choices we make about our time? Are we willing to give God control of our time and our lives? Are we able to let some things go and not try to cram every activity into one day? Our actions declare who it is that we believe is in control of our lives—God or us. God not only gives us our time and lives, but calls us to vocations through which we exercise our gifts and talents.[10]

Life presents too much pressure and too many opportunities for us to do everything. When we allow our lives to be overloaded by options, we can get pulled in too many directions and can lack the energy and focus to enjoy our main activities and give them our best. We cannot do everything well at once. Therefore, we must cut out some activities so we can focus on the most important ones.

When possible, it helps if we can develop a comfort with how much money we have. I have sat with many people who have no choice but to work more than they would like just to get by. Yet many other people find themselves working harder than they should simply out of the desire for more money. When we keep our lives limited and controlled, we are more likely to live in balance. It is easier to balance a more limited number of activities than to try to keep numerous balls in the air.

The question arises then, how can we learn to set priorities and say no? I have found four ideas that help in this process. First, realize that experience helps. We have to practice saying no. As we mature, we will naturally get better at discerning which activities will yield fruit and which distractions can be cut out, and we will gain confidence in making hard choices.

Second, realize that *no* is not a bad word. Many people in our congregations will respect us for knowing our limits. For pastors and other congregational leaders, the reluctance to say no can be a problem. Many congregational leaders are people pleasers at heart. We don't like to disappoint others. Early in my career, it would pain me to turn down a request for a meeting or an invitation to speak somewhere. Then a wise nurse from our parish convinced me that people respect us more when we know and explain our limits. Besides, God has given gifts to many people throughout the church, so we all can share in the work. I soon realized that I hadn't been given every gift in the world because I wasn't meant to do all the work. By saying no more frequently, I could share both the burden and the joy of being in ministry with others. I have had to say no to officiating at events, speaking opportunities, and appearing places that I'd otherwise like to as pastor. I don't attend all church meetings. I've had to say no to some mission projects. I have had to work hard to achieve this, but it is important. The medieval theologian Meister Eckhart put it this way, "God is found in the soul not by adding anything, but by a process of subtraction."

Third, realize that, through our gifts and callings, God gives us clues about what activities we should focus on. Everyone has different gifts. The abilities with which God has entrusted us offer signs about which activities we should pursue. Following a calling means pursuing some activities to the exclusion of others. A quotation from John Calvin that was included earlier bears repeating here. Calvin wrote:

> The Lord bids each one of us in all life's actions to look to his calling. For He knows with what great restlessness human nature flames, with what fickleness it is born hither and thither, how its ambition longs to embrace various things at once. Therefore, lest through our stupidity and rashness everything be turned topsy-turvy, he has appointed duties for every man in his particular way of life. And that no one may thoughtlessly transgress his limits, he has named these various kinds of living "callings." Therefore each individual has his own kind of living assigned to him by the Lord as a sort of sentry post so that he may not needlessly wander about throughout life. . . .[11]

Calvin thought each Christian should listen to God, determine his or her calling, and say no to distractions. He wrote further, "We must take heed that we do not turn our thoughts or our minds to any other activity but, on the contrary, endeavor to be free from every distraction and apply ourselves exclusively to God's calling."[12] Realizing that God means for us to do some things and not others makes it easier to say no to some opportunities, because we are being true to God when we do so.

Fourth, realize that taking stock of our gifts through prayer and reflection can help. I have in my journal this list: (1) pray, (2) listen to your heart and what gives satisfaction, (3) write down where your strengths lie, and (4) think about how you have made a difference for others. These four guideposts help me think about how to use my time so that my lifestyle is consistent with God's will. When I am thinking about the variety of activities and options before me, I can examine them in light of my list and callings. I find it easier to say no to things that don't line up with my list or God's callings for my life.

God has given each of us the ability to do many things. Yet, we have to make choices, to say no to some activities in order to do well the things God has called us to. Using our time wisely requires focus and discipline. While it can be difficult to make choices, setting priorities can make a big difference in work-life balance.

Pastor Rick Warren once noted, "Whenever I used to see one of my mentors, Peter Drucker, he would say, 'Don't tell me what new things you're doing. Tell me what you've stopped doing.' The mark of leadership is often knowing what not to do."[13] Warren concluded, "You can't do everything. And God doesn't expect you to."[14] When we set limits, close some doors, and refrain from overloading our lives, we are better able to balance them.

For Reflection

1. Can you simplify your life? If so, how?
2. What are you called to in life?
3. What has your life experience taught you about saying no?
4. Pray about what gives you satisfaction, where your strengths lie, and how you have made a difference in the lives of others. What does this reflection tell you about how God is calling you and about what activities to prioritize?
5. If you had to cut out three activities from your life now, what would they be? How would you go about saying no to them?

MAKING REST A HIGH PRIORITY

Rest in the Lord, and wait patiently for him.
                                        —Psalm 37:7 (KJV)

At the service when I was installed as the pastor of Bradley Hills Presbyterian Church, a good friend gave the "charge" to me as the new pastor. Traditionally, the charge is the advice given to the new pastor about how to live and be in ministry. What stood out most to me was my friend's call to remember that, although I was following Jesus, I "was not Jesus." That was an important reminder. We are too often tempted in work to do "everything," as if we were the messiah of our congregation or organization. My friend helped me realize how important it is for me to let go, go home, and rest in order to live with balance. Yet it can be so difficult.

When I was growing up, my grandfather, H. C. VanKirk, used to tell me, "The art of relaxation is the greatest of all arts." My grandfather knew that we often find it difficult to relax, yet it's vitally important. As Henry David Thoreau said, "Life is too short to be in a hurry."[15]

When we seek to change our thinking about how we spend our time and energy to take more seriously our need for rest, one theological principle that helps is sanctification. From the Latin word *sanctus* ("holy") comes *sanctification* or *holiness,* the idea that God makes us more like Christ as we grow in our relationship with God. The Holy Spirit can help us develop healthy patterns despite the pressures of the world. Some people have joined monastic orders to find real separation from the pressures and influences of our modern world. For congregational leaders who serve churches and live with those pressures and influences every day, finding time for rejuvenation, recreation, and renewal during evening times, on Sunday, or other Sabbath, and on vacation is essential.

Scholar Joshua Stanton writes of sanctification in Judaism:

> Sanctification may be understood within the Jewish tradition as "chosenness." This idea is often directly connected to the Exodus from Egypt or the Jewish forefathers. Chosenness, as manifested through the revelation of the Torah to Moses at Mount Sinai, resulted in a set of laws that guide our actions and enable us to lead meaningful lives and by extension make full use of our God-given abilities therein. The Jewish precept of sanctification

is palpable in nearly every prayer. *"Ki Banu Bacharta . . ."* because you chose our children we are blessed with the Sabbath, Jews recount in the *Kiddish* prayer before settling down to their meals on the eve of *Shabbat (Erev Shabbat)*.[16]

In the Reformed tradition, John Calvin wrote of sanctification:

> . . . we must bear in mind that Christ came endowed with the Holy Spirit . . . to separate us from the world and to gather us unto the hope of the eternal inheritance. Hence he is called the "spirit of sanctification" (2 Thess. 2:13; 1 Pet. 1:2; Rom. 1:4) because he not only quickens and nourishes us by a general power that is visible both in the human race and in the rest of the living creatures, but he is also the root and seed of heavenly life in us.[17]

Being sanctified as God's people, Calvin taught, means adopting an attitude that flows from our understanding of God's will, even if such an understanding conflicts with mainstream culture. He wrote that people "cannot properly worship without dedicating themselves to him [God] in such a way that they separate themselves from the world."[18] We should not take ourselves or our work too seriously. To live as sanctified people, we must live as if rest matters to us. Because we are sanctified people, we are free to rest. *Rest* is not a "four-letter word." Part of the notion of sanctification, particularly for Protestants in the Reformed tradition, holds that life is a journey that is never quite completed. We are works in progress. Although a "work ethic" culture might define people by what they accomplish, our actions and works will not save us ultimately. The theology of grace that was so important to Calvin allows Christians to leave their salvation to God. God saves us by grace through faith. That promise should free us from working too hard and allow us to rest in God's grace.

Our model for balance comes through the life of Jesus Christ. Contrast Jesus' actions with those of other well-regarded Christians, such as Calvin or even Paul, who wrote much of the

New Testament. Calvin did not live in the moment; he was far from being a man of leisure. He was bi-vocational, multitasking, and overworked. Yet Calvin was at least interested in rest, even if he didn't live out his words. He once said, "Nothing is more desirable than a tranquil mind."[19] Paul was a type-A person, too. He was bi-vocational, pursuing both tent-making and ministry, and went on several missionary journeys. About the only time Paul was at rest was when he was forced to be—when he was in jail! Even there he was at work writing.

How did Jesus live? Jesus was deliberate about the way he used time. He knew that his work was of vital importance and that his days on earth would end soon. Yet Jesus rested. He took time by himself. He was not afraid to separate from people for a time. He was in the world, but separated from it. Jesus became so sought after that he had a hard time getting away from crowds. However, Jesus took periods of purposeful rest within his broader ministry. Consider these passages:

- Matthew 11:28-30: "Come to me, all you that are weary and are carrying heavy burdens, and I will give you rest. Take my yoke upon you, and learn from me; for I am gentle and humble in heart, and you will find rest for your souls. For my yoke is easy, and my burden is light."
- Matthew 17:1: "Six days later, Jesus took with him Peter and James and his brother John and led them up a high mountain, by themselves."
- Mark 1:35: "In the morning, while it was still very dark, he got up and went out to a deserted place, and there he prayed."
- Mark 6:30-32: "The apostles gathered around Jesus, and told him all they had done and taught. He said to them, "Come away to a deserted place all by yourselves and rest a while." For many were coming and going, and they had no leisure even to eat. And they went away in the boat to a deserted place by themselves."
- Luke 6:12: "Now during those days he went out to the mountain to pray; and he spent the night in prayer to God."
- Luke 9:10: "On their return the apostles told Jesus all they had done. He took them with him and withdrew privately to a city called Bethsaida."

Why did Jesus rest? Jesus was fully human and fully divine, so perhaps he needed to rest—or perhaps he did not. Jesus certainly modeled rest for us, however, as God did on the seventh day of creation. God rested then, not because God needed to rejuvenate, but to set aside time as holy. Christians can look to God's revelation to learn how to act by following the example of Jesus in his rest. We need to trust God and follow our model in Jesus. In order to live in this world, but not be strictly of this world—in order to find balance in life—congregational leaders, and all people, need rest.

The word *rest* means both "relaxation" and "remainder." It suggests rejuvenation and recreation, as well as a time where we fully separate ourselves from work. Christians need both longer and shorter periods of rest. For example, on the "seventh day," after all God's works of creation, God rested for a time period that became known as the Sabbath. Or we might rest for only a short time, perhaps praying for fifteen minutes. The word also can mean what we do with the "rest" of the time between periods of work. As Jesus said, "Seek first the kingdom of God and the rest will be given to you" (Matthew 6:33). This second kind of rest time might not allow for complete relaxation, but it can still be rejuvenating.

Practically speaking, recognizing the value of rest can help congregational leaders avoid burnout. Congregational leaders need short and longer periods of rest. Even if shorter breaks do not allow the full relaxation longer ones do, they have great value. Some shorter periods of rest may require concentration—engaging one's mind and spirit in Scripture reading, meditation, or prayer, for example—yet these times relax us, draw us closer to God, and help us live with a spirit of holiness. It can be difficult to take a break for prayer each day or to begin each morning reading Scripture rather than the newspaper. Yet those moments help Christians live with more balance. When the pressures of life make it difficult for me to take longer periods of rest, I have found that praying for an hour—or even for just ten or fifteen minutes—can greatly help me.

We must learn to sleep for the seven to eight hours medical professionals tell us we require each night, to honor the Sabbath, and to value vacations. Having a full day of rest can help re-create us. Too many pastors fail to observe the Sabbath or to take their vacations. I find I have to really focus on taking my weekly Sabbath time. Much as God rested from all God's works, we need to find time when we rest fully from our work. Congregational leaders also need weeklong (or longer) vacations during the year to be rejuvenated. Long breaks—perhaps three or even thirty days for a retreat, for example—can be very nourishing. Making rest a high priority is important to work-life balance.

For Reflection

1. In what ways are you able to separate yourself from the pressures of life and culture?
2. How do you define *rest*? Where do you find it? Who are your role models in rest?
3. Finish completing and reflect upon the results of the Tell Yourself about Your Time chart in Appendix 2.

Rethinking What We Mean by Balance

You must ruthlessly eliminate hurry from your life, for hurry is the great enemy of spiritual life in our world today.
—Dallas Willard, Senior Fellow, Trinity Forum. In Cherie Harder, "A Time to Be Ruthless," *The Trinity Forum Update.* (October 28, 2010)

Too often when people talk with me about "work-life balance," their focus is on making sure they are not working so hard at the office that they lack sufficient time with their families. We have already established that this is a critical part of the equation. But what is missing from such an understanding of balance is the recognition that, for most of us, just getting home to take care of someone else does not sufficiently take care of our own needs. If we fill every hour that we are away from our jobs with caregiving responsibilities, we are still going to be exhausted. I know too many people who seem to believe the goal of work-life balance is to fill every moment with either a work activity, a family obligation, or a caregiving activity. For them, "balance" is no more than a way to pack in as much activity as possible. The result of this approach is that people run themselves ragged.

While we should not make idols of ourselves, we are called by God to take care of ourselves. Self-care is a theological value. It may not sound theological, but we find our motivation for it in our faith tradition. If Christians believe in *imago dei*, the concept that we are made in the image of God, then we are responsible to God to care for ourselves as part of God's creation. The writer of the Book of Genesis emphasizes several times that humanity is made in God's image. Moreover, the Synoptic Gospel writers record Jesus' statement that we should treat others as we ourselves would like to be treated. Mark's recording of the Golden Rule, the "second great commandment," is that followers of God should "love your neighbor as yourself" (12:31). This statement implies that we should love ourselves. Taking good and proper care of oneself is important theologically. Self-care honors God's creation and Jesus' commandment.

The resources of the church can help us do that. Through adult education, preaching, and modeling of healthy behaviors, congregational leaders can help encourage people to include sufficient time for rest and activities that give them energy. In fact, many activities that churches have traditionally taught, such as prayer, meditation, Scripture reading, and worship, can be restful and can give us energy. Moreover, activities such as yoga, exercise, and journaling, which some congregations now encourage, can also contribute to such balance. Churches are well positioned to influence members and visitors to understand balance as including enough time for rest and rejuvenation.

Too often, people think that work-life balance is the same as work-family balance. Many people hope to spend some time at their job and some time with their children, seeking to "balance" these activities as if they were on opposite sides of a scale. However, such a mindset misses the fact that both paid employment and caregiving are challenging. Work outside the home and work inside the home can both be difficult and very tiring. No matter how much we love our job or our families, they both take energy. We need other activities that provide refreshment. That is why I prefer to think in terms of striving for balance between work— both paid and unpaid caregiving—and life—the activities of rest and rejuvenation, as proper self-care.

A person who labors many hours outside the home is working, but so is a parent who primarily spends time caring for a child, or a daughter or son who cares for an aging parent. For them, "family" *is* "work." Raising a family is hard work. Sure, it's rewarding, but it's also frustrating, maddening, and, at times, exasperating. I often deal with difficult situations in my job; yet I find that my toddlers can provoke feelings of frustration in me I didn't know I had. Children do not come with an instruction manual. When my wife and I had our first child, we were overwhelmed. He needed to be changed. He woke up at night. We had so much trouble getting our first child to sleep that we would walk him around outside at night in a stroller. Caring for elderly parents can be equally difficult. In fact, I know many folks, myself included, who at times take comfort in the relative rest and relaxation available at the office as compared to the many demands we experience at home.

We need to add another category to our analysis—"family-life balance"—to parallel work-life balance. Sometimes family responsibilities can give us energy, much as work responsibilities sometimes can. However, family responsibilities are often difficult and draining. The challenge of work-family balance is that both work and family responsibilities can be very tiring—so "balancing" the two against each other is not really possible. Rather than work and family balancing each other, they fall on the same side of the scale. I believe *life* is a better term to use in describing what provides balance. "Life" provides balance to both work and family. The real balance is not between work and family. The real balance is between activities that *take* our energy (and these may include work and family responsibilities, however rewarding they may be) and activities that *give* us energy.

I think of people as the scales themselves, trying to hold up both work and family responsibilities so that life can be lived to the fullest. The question is: What is holding up the scales that are weighed down by both work and family obligations? Where can we turn for energy, rejuvenation, health, and strength to meet our work and family commitments? This is a question that both clergy and the people sitting in the pews on Sunday mornings are asking.

Christianity, like most other religious traditions, teaches disciplines that calm and focus people, helping them to find emotional and spiritual energy and strength. That is one reason religion can be valuable in helping people experience more balance in life. Religious people are often involved in discussions about work-life balance in boardrooms, in human resource meetings, in the research departments of universities, and around kitchen tables. It is time religious institutions become part of the solution to the societal problem of work-life balance. Congregations can help their members and visitors see the connection between healthy life practices (including spiritual disciplines) and work-life balance. Congregational leaders need to communicate that the spiritual practices of the church are not only important for religious obser-vance but can help with work-life pressures as well.

Balance means setting aside enough time for energy-giving activities that do not involve work or caregiving responsibilities, so that one can be rejuvenated for those obligations and can enjoy life. I have found that spiritual activities—such as prayer, meditation, Scripture reading, worship, yoga, exercise, and journaling—are the most helpful. I include yoga, exercise, and journaling because I have found them to be profoundly spiritual activities. These prac-tices can help Christians find rejuvenation and connect to God in ways different from Sunday worship. We've started a yoga ministry at the last two churches I have served. I try to write in my journal in the evenings. I typically exercise in some way thirty minutes most days. Each of these activities strengthens my spirit and provides rest for my body and soul. I also experience the presence of the Holy Spirit in such activities, especially when I begin or end them with Scripture reading and prayer. For example, during one summer in our current yoga ministry, I read from the Psalms and prayed to close each session. One role of congregational leaders is to help the people in our churches realize that self-care matters and that work-life balance should include activities that provide the rest and energy needed so we can meet our obligations and feel spiritually alive.

For Reflection

1. Where do you find energy in your life?
2. Does your family time usually seem relaxing or is it often as stressful as your employed work time?
3. At what times in life have you felt the most in balance? What factors made these times feel balanced?
4. What spiritual activities most contribute to your sense of self-care?

BEING INTENTIONAL ABOUT HOW WE USE OUR TIME

> We live and we die by time. And we must not commit the
> sin of losing our track on time.
> —Chuck Noland, *Castaway* (20th Century Fox, 2000)

At its core, work-life balance is about how we use our time. Psychologist Tim Kasser writes about what he calls "time affluence"—the feeling that we have enough time to complete everything we want to do.[20] Kasser contends that this is a critical component of human well-being. Time poverty, on the other hand, is our feeling "stressed, rushed, overworked, and behind."[21] Feeling relaxed and having a sense that we have enough time to do what must be done is an important attitude in a balanced life.

Fortunately, our faith can help us here. The Bible was written during a period when the understanding of "time" was largely based on natural events, such as the rising and setting of the sun, the waxing and waning of the moon, and the changing of the seasons. Time was about rhythmic cycles, not precise moments. The length of time changed from day to day. Sunrise and sunset occur at different times each day, so the length of the Sabbath, for example, would vary from week to week and place to place. This contrasts with the modern sense of time, which defines a day as an exact twenty-four-hour period.

The New Testament contains more than 140 references to "time." The Hebrew Bible includes many more.[22] There are several words for time in each testament, but the most frequently used terms in both Hebrew *(eth)* and Greek *(kairos)* share three important qualities. First, time in the Bible is more about the content of each moment than about its duration. The difference between the biblical view and the modern view of time can be seen in how a person might understand the amount of time needed for a meeting. Today, for example, a person might schedule a meeting to last from "noon to 2:00 p.m."—the length of time people will sit face to face and work together. However, a person using the biblical view of time might call a meeting to last "as long as needed to plan the mission project and the Advent party." Such thinking focuses on the content of the meeting rather than the temporal length of it.

I think the difference between the way we look at time today and the understanding of time in the biblical eras parallels the differing roles of time in the sports of football and baseball. In a football game, teams compete for a specific amount of time— four fifteen-minute quarters. In baseball, the game usually lasts nine innings, with each team remaining at bat until the opposing team gets three outs—nine times. A baseball game can take ninety minutes or more than four hours. The game lasts as long as it takes to complete the activity. The baseball game, like biblical time, is defined by what is occurring, not by the number of minutes left on a clock.

Second, biblical time is ordered. Biblical people were more connected than we are to the sun, moon, land, weather, and outdoors; to the daily coming and going of light and dark; and to the passage of seasons. These connections led people to see time as ordered, even as it is also about what is occurring. We may have lost some of that connection today since our electric lights and heat and air conditioning all reduce the impact of the daily and seasonal rhythms of time.

Third, time is connected to God.[23] People in biblical times believed there was a right time for each activity and that God was the one who ordered the seasons, appointed each activity to its time, and had a hand in guiding what happened in the world.[24] God's gift of Sabbath demonstrates the biblical characteristics of time. Sabbath, which traditionally followed the disappearance of light, is the original principle of work-life balance.[25] In the Book of Genesis, God instituted work-life balance by working at creation for six days and then resting for one day. By working for six days and resting for one, God was being intentional about the use of time. Within the biblical story of the creation of the world, time is ordered by periods of both work and rest, and time is connected to God. In it, God modeled intentionality in planning time. Christians and Jews know from the Fourth Commandment that we are instructed to set a day apart and to rest one day a week as God did. We are to have one day a week to be freed to focus intently on the content of activities. The theological principle of Sabbath exemplifies the biblical idea of time.

Perhaps the most important decision we mortals can make is to think carefully about how we spend the time we have. We tend to plan time for work and time for rest more seriously and intentionally when we view our time on earth as finite and ordered, and as a gift from God. In order to incorporate the activities that provide energy, many of us must rethink our use of time. Even if we say no and cut out unnecessary activities, most of us have too many obligations and cannot just ignore the clock.

Most days, I spend the morning rushing to get dressed, to eat breakfast, to get our girls changed, and to get our boys dressed, fed, and out the door to school. It can be so hectic that I sometimes forget to bring my son's lunch to school and have to return home to get it. Life is too often about rushing from one activity to another. Many families face similar challenges. I know so many people for whom time is short.

The writer of Ecclesiastes reminds us there is a time for everything. "A time to be born and a time to die. A time to laugh and a time to weep. A time to plant and a time to pluck up what is planted" (3:3). Time is not an open book on which we can write whatever we want.[26] We have schedules. We are responsible to others. Some things in life happen only during certain seasons.

Yet we often wish we could control time. Consider the conversation between Alice and the Mad Hatter in *Alice in Wonderland:*

"If you knew Time as well as I do," said the Hatter, "you wouldn't talk about wasting *it*. It's *him*."

"I don't know what you mean," said Alice.

"Of course you don't!" the Hatter said, tossing his head contemptuously. "I dare say you never even spoke to Time!"

"Perhaps not," Alice cautiously replied, "but I know I have to beat time when I learn music."

"Ah! that accounts for it," said the Hatter. "He won't stand beating. Now, if you only kept on good terms with him, he'd do almost anything you liked with the clock. For instance, suppose it were nine o'clock in the morning, just time to begin lessons: you'd only have to whisper a hint to Time, and round goes the clock in a twinkling! Half-past one, time for dinner!" . . .

"That would be grand, certainly," said Alice thoughtfully. . . ."[27]

The Mad Hatter portrays time as a person, one who can be influenced to extend the time to be allotted for a person's favorite activities if that person got to know him. Yet we know time cannot be stretched or changed. Each hour has sixty minutes. Each day has twenty-four hours. Most years have 365 days.

God is ultimately in control of time. Time started before we got here, and time will continue after we graduate to heaven. Yes, we do occasionally enjoy unexpected gifts of "extra" time. Those who live in northern climates begin each winter knowing it might snow hard some days, and school or work will be cancelled. "Snow days" can be unexpected gifts of Sabbath time. Perhaps we will decide to cancel a trip at the last minute and gain a free weekend we didn't expect. We might decide to let go of thinking about the clock for a bit. It is possible we might develop a new schedule that acts as a liberating restriction for us, one that frees us to live more fully in the present. For many of us, it's about time.

For Reflection

1. Do you see a connection between living in the moment and living with balance? If so, how can you order your days so you can live more in the moment?
2. How does your understanding of time inform your work-life balance?

CHAPTER 5

We Need to Change Our Habits

Do one thing at a time. Give each experience all your
attention. Try to resist being distracted by other sights and
sounds, other thoughts and tasks, and when it is, guide
your mind back to what you're doing.
　　　　　　　　　—John Walsh, author and art historian,
　　　　　　　　　　　Speech at Wheaton College, 2000

If we truly wish to make balance a high priority, we need to
develop healthy rituals. Practicing healthy habits over and over
helps us internalize them until they become part of our perma-
nent behavior.[1]

The four attitudes discussed in chapter 4 can lead to specific
changes that will aid us in achieving more balance in life. Learning
to say no can help us manage our relationship with technology.
Making rest a high priority can motivate us to honor weekly and
daily Sabbath. Emphasizing self-care within our understanding
of "balance" can lead us to develop healthier personal practices.
Being intentional about our use of time can help us set healthy
schedules.

Why I Don't Own a Smartphone

The separation of work and home is one thing that babies
born in 2011 will never know.
—Stacy Johnson, *Money Talks News,* January 5, 2011[2]

In the last few decades, continuing developments in communication and information technologies have changed the way we work
and live. Most of us have access to devices—cellphones, smartphones, personal digital assistants, tablets, and computers—that
can tie us to work even when we are not physically present at the
workplace. Technology itself is neutral. It can help or hurt work-
life balance. A recently released survey by Deloitte found that 60
percent of employees believe technology plays an important role
in helping them meet their professional and personal demands
while still caring for children and meeting other obligations.[3]
However, the proliferation of these communication devices can
make finding work-life balance today a particular challenge. They
can keep us from being mentally and emotionally present with our
friends, families, children, and self even when we are physically
with them.

It takes discipline to say no to the constant connection with
work that new technologies offer. Laptops, cell phones, and the
Internet allow us greater flexibility to respond to work needs
without going to the office, but they also make it harder for many
of us to separate work and family time. Forty percent of American
workers say they use technology for their jobs during non-work
hours.[4] Furthermore, we are not always wired to the office by
choice. Over one-fifth of workers say they are required to be
accessible to their employers during non-work hours.[5] By some
estimates, this increased access adds up to a full month of extra
work annually beyond the tasks performed during standard office
hours.[6]

In addition to blurring the line between work and life, these
technologies intrude in our lives in other ways. Former finance

columnist for the *Washington Post,* Nancy Trejos, explains by describing her situation: "One of my longest, most stable relationships over the past three years has not been with a boyfriend. It's been with my BlackBerry. . . . It is, without fail, the last thing I look at when I go to sleep and the first thing I look at when I wake up."[7] During my vacation to Cape Cod in August 2010, my father-in-law showed me a picture he called "Texting from Monomoy." It was a picture of a family member walking along a beautiful beach with incredible birds all around and water lapping on the shore—and she was missing the whole scene because she was texting on her phone.

In *Hamlet's BlackBerry: A Practical Philosophy for Building a Good Life in the Digital Age,* Williams Powers explains that our concern about the role of technology in our lives is not new.[8] He writes that all new communication technologies over time—from the written scroll to the printing press to books to TV to the Internet to smartphones—have provoked similar anxieties. Powers suggests that some people in Plato's era feared that the ability to write words on a written scroll would reduce the amount of face time people had with others, for if one could receive the thoughts of others by something other than conversation, it could impact the "life of the mind."[9] Powers notes that Henry David Thoreau was similarly concerned about the impact the telegraph might have in "pulling people away from life's most meaningful experiences, including the family dinner table."[10]

We must learn to control technology or it will control us. This can be difficult. When we try and break free from our addiction to technology, we may experience withdrawal symptoms. In a 2010 survey, one thousand students in ten countries were asked to abstain from social media for twenty-four hours. When asked to describe how they felt, they used words such as "miserable, anxious, jittery, and crazy."[11]

However, hope is not lost. If Christians take seriously the value of saying no, we can learn to control technology. Some smartphones allow users to switch between personal and work modes.

Some families go on "text-free vacations," leaving the laptops and cellphones at home.[12] One company even offers "digital detox retreats."[13] Nancy Trejos explains that for her own retreat, she checked into the "tranquility suite" at the Hotel Monaco in Chicago where one has to put one's electronic devices in a locked safe box in the office for the stay. For the first two days, Trejos found herself struggling with withdrawal. But by the third day of detox, she started to enjoy it. She found that she had to communicate with people "the old fashioned way"—face to face.[14] Plato and Thoreau would have approved. Imagine if we communicated more face to face.

I wish I had the strength to do as Trejos did and not spend so much time on my computer (ironically, I think this as I write this sentence on my computer), but I remain a work in progress. One decision I did make in 2005 was to give up my smartphone. When I worked in government I had one—and I used it constantly. I used it to send and receive e-mails, to make calls, to access the Internet, and to play video games. I was addicted, and I needed to break free from it to be able to live more fully in the moment. My decision to give up my smartphone was important for me. Even today, I don't carry a BlackBerry, an iPhone, or any other smartphone or personal digital assistant. I have a cell phone, but I turn it off frequently, and I am selective about when I answer it (only my wife's calls are always picked up). I feel it's important for me not to have a smartphone at this time, because I don't want to be accessible at every moment, and I don't want to be addicted to my technology.

For me, the issue is one of boundaries. The boundaries I am able to set by not having a smartphone and being at least somewhat inaccessible make a big difference for me. They have helped me be more present with my family and friends. Saying no to certain technologies has made me more efficient at work and helped me to maintain my schedule. That has given me confidence to say no in other areas of life so I am less overloaded. It has helped me better keep my commitments.

For Reflection

1. What role does technology play in your life?
2. Do you feel technology helps or hurts your work-life balance?
3. Try a "digital detox," giving up your electronic devices for seventy-two hours this week. Then take time to reflect on the experience. How did it feel? Did it help you?
4. What else in your life do you need to say no to?

WHY WAIT FOR THE WEEKEND?

> Teach me the art of taking minute vacations, of slowing down . . .
>
> —Wilfred A. Peterson, "Slow Me Down, Lord,"
> *The Art of Living Treasure Chest* (New York:
> Simon and Schuster, 1977), 63

The story is told of two men who had to clear a field of trees. The contract called for them to be paid per tree. Bill wanted the day to be profitable, so he grunted and sweated, swinging his ax relentlessly. Ed, on the other hand, seemed to be working about half as fast. He even took a rest and sat off to the side for a few minutes. Bill kept chopping away until every muscle and tendon in his body was screaming. At the end of the day, Bill was terribly sore, but Ed was smiling and telling jokes. What's more, Ed had cut down more trees. Bill said, "I noticed you were sitting while I worked without a break. How did you cut down more trees than I did?" Smiling, Ed said, "Did you not notice I was sharpening my ax while I was sitting?"

Many of us might view Ed's wisdom with interest, for the boundaries between work and rest in U.S. culture have blurred. A generation or two ago, many Americans would work each weekday but could easily put away work in the evenings, on weekends, or on vacations. But as the boundaries go away, we need daily disciplines to counter the pervasive impacts of work-life imbalance. In chapter 4, I explained how the gift of the Sabbath showed that God intended us to use time for both work and for rest. Taking seriously our rest times and the boundaries we set helps us stay sharp for the tasks ahead. In the midst of life's busyness, the underlying theology of Sabbath can help. It holds that God cares about how we spend our time and that significant time away from work can draw us closer to God. It can help us take a disciplined approach to balancing our work and energy in and out of the home. Yet many of us find it tremendously difficult to honor the Sabbath fully and to make our rest a priority by resting for a full day each week. Keeping the Sabbath is a challenge with the ever-creeping demands of work and of family.

Ministers face an additional challenge. Because pastors work on Sundays, "keeping Sabbath" means we must take another day each week free from labor. It is hard to work on Sunday and rest on a weekday when the rest of the culture follows a different schedule. For pastors, working on Sundays often means giving up socializing on Saturday evenings, not being able to go away on weekends, and working evenings when family and friends have free time. Having a different schedule from spouses also makes planning family trips difficult. It remains a major struggle in my own life. For me, Sabbath time comes on Saturday, a day I try to guard for family time as much as I can. Many clergy I know have only one day off of work each week, and in that day they often run errands and do chores rather than observing an uninterrupted time of rest. For clergy, given the pressures to work six days a week, mini or daily Sabbaths can be particularly important. Having a weekly Sabbath is important; but including times of Sabbath each day can be especially helpful to those who have trouble protecting a weekly Sabbath.

I believe Christian theology and tradition support daily as well as weekly Sabbaths as part of our staying connected to Christ. As we have discussed, God's Fourth Commandment reads: "Remember the Sabbath day and keep it holy. Six days you shall labor and do all your work. But the seventh day is a Sabbath to the Lord your God; you shall not do any work" (Exodus 20:4). One translation of the Hebrew goes further and suggests that God's people should "guard" the Sabbath. God has made it a holy day, and we should honor that. On the Sabbath, God rested from all God's works. It is important for us to set aside a full day for rest each week to follow God's command as much as we can. Most Christians today honor the resurrection by observing the Sabbath on Sunday, the first day of the week, rather than on Saturday, the last day. But we can also honor Jesus by remembering that he also included moments of prayer and solitude within the midst of his activities. Jesus went into the wilderness for forty days, resisting great temptations, before beginning his public ministry. Jesus also rested, not from all his works, but through moments of prayerful rejuvenation within the busyness of his activities.

For the ancient Israelites in exile in Babylon, far from the location of the temple that had unified them, observing weekly Sabbath helped strengthen their identity as a set-apart people. Christians, by definition, find their identity in Jesus Christ. John Calvin wrote about how Jesus is the constant embodiment and true completion of Sabbath: "Still there can be no doubt that, on the advent of our Lord, Jesus Christ, the ceremonial part of the [fourth] commandment was abolished. He is the truth. . . . He, I say, is the true completion of the Sabbath."[15] Through Christ, God makes available a holy identity for Christians in the same way that the Israelites found their holy identity in the weekly Sabbath. In the eleventh century, Pope Alexander II argued that "the Trinity in its fullness is honored every day of the church year."[16] I believe that our connection with God through Christ is maximized when, in rest, we seek to commune with Christ each day.

The idea of daily Sabbath is supported by the Reformed tradition. Many Reformers, such as Calvin, Richard Baxter, and John Bailey, developed their own types of daily Sabbath emphases.

Calvin wrote, "If men were able on their own strength to fulfill the law, he (God) would have said to them, 'Work!' But on the contrary he said, 'Rest in order that God might work.'"[17] Calvin also believed that Christians could find new rest in Jesus Christ—extending the benefits of the weekly Sabbath to each day. Calvin wrote, "The resurrection of our Lord (is) the end and accomplishment of that true rest which the ancient Sabbath typified."[18] Calvin wrote further, "We here begin our blessed rest in him, and daily make new progress in it."[19] Calvin felt that the promise of God to the Israelites was fulfilled in the coming of Christ, who allowed them and allows us to enjoy the promised rest on every day, not just one.[20] Calvin's writings remind us that we are to reflect each day on the eternal Sabbath God has prepared for us and that each day we can find our rest in Christ. Reflecting on Hebrews 4:7-10, Calvin wrote, "There is a sabbathizing reserved for God's people, that is, a spiritual rest, to which God daily invites us."[21]

I have found it helpful to practice some form of spiritual rest each day. These can include making sure I am home to eat dinner with family, going to bed on time, having moments of prayer, reading Scripture, being disciplined about taking breaks from work every hour or two, making a realistic to-do list at the beginning of each day, or just having the strength to put down a pen, laptop, or other tools, and relax in the middle of the day.

We all have unique responsibilities—which may include some combination of paid work, home maintenance, child and elder care, and volunteer activities. The challenge for each of us is to develop personal criteria that will help us determine what we'll do with our Sabbath time. That is, we need to decide which activities we consider "work" and which are "rest." Those activities that clearly take energy from me I consider work. That means they not only take energy to do but also leave me tired. Even though I love ministry, after several hours on a workday or by Sunday after a long workweek, I feel my work activities taking energy from me. Activities that give me energy include prayer, sleep, exercise, conversations with friends, and watching movies. When we are particularly busy, we must be disciplined both to complete those tasks we have no choice about doing and to ensure we take enough time for rest.

The real challenge is thinking about those activities that lie in the middle. Cooking, yard work, child care, and ministry all give me energy at some times and take energy from me at others. For example, after our twin daughters were born, my wife and I often felt overwhelmed by the responsibility of caring for two infants. But I tried not to do activities that took my energy, either paid work or household chores, after their bedtime. Sticking with that required discipline, but when I started to think of my daily use of time as part of my worship of God, that helped elevate my decisions about my time to a new level.

Although paying attention to our energy and what makes us happy is important and can give us good clues about balance, the genius of Sabbath is that it can help us stay ahead of ourselves. Working non-stop for a time and then collapsing does not do our bodies and spirits as much good as does maintaining the balance that comes from observing the God-instituted weekly Sabbath as well as daily Sabbaths. Such Sabbath practices can help us leave behind activities that will end up taking our energy, no matter how much we love them, in favor of those activities that give us energy. As we'll see later in this chapter, having a daily schedule can help us ensure that we honor the Sabbaths needed to maintain our energy.

Henry Ward Beecher once wrote, "A world without a Sabbath would be like a man without a smile, like a summer without flowers, and like a homestead without a garden."[22] While I don't always achieve it, my goal each day is to spend a minimum of ten minutes reading Scripture, twenty minutes in prayer or silence, thirty minutes on exercise, and fifteen minutes journaling. These daily moments of "mini-Sabbath" make a great difference to me. I would urge you to discover what it is that gives you energy, and then let Sabbath be both a weekly and a daily activity. Honor God's commandment, Christ's modeling of rest in his own life, and God's creation of you through self-care by elevating the importance of rest in your life.

For Reflection

1. Do you observe the Sabbath each week? If not, why not?
2. Do you take all your vacation time each year? If not, why not?
3. What changes could you make to begin taking more time for rest?
4. How do you find daily rest?
5. Observe Sabbath this week. Reflect in a journal on how you felt observing Sabbath.

CARING FOR OURSELVES

Seek first the kingdom of wealth, and you'll worry over every dollar. . . . Seek first the kingdom of popularity, and you'll relive every conflict. Seek first the kingdom of safety, and you'll jump at every crack of the twig. But seek first His kingdom, and you will find it . . . and never worry.
—Max Lucado, *Fearless: Imagining Your Life Without Fear* (Nashville: Thomas Nelson, 2009), 51

Achieving a healthy work-life balance eventually comes down to personal responsibility and discipline. We must make the right choices, and our choices must be influenced by our attitudes and values. Behaviors that flow from our deeply held beliefs help us counter external pressures that keep us from taking care of ourselves.

Public policy can provide opportunities for balance, but only personal responsibility allows us to capitalize on those opportunities. Community groups, day care centers, and relatives can take weight off the shoulders of families, but only personal responsibility ensures that we use wisely the time gained. No matter how much support our employers, our nation's public policies, or our families may give us, the ways we use the free time and space those supports provide determine how balanced our lives are.

Establishing healthy practices can help both clergy and lay leaders avoid burnout. While congregations may push their leaders to meet all their needs all the time, when church leaders are balanced and refreshed, they are much better able to serve and lead their congregations over time. Through adult educational programs and other offerings, churches can help their members implement ideas that can improve their well-being. This can lead to healthier members, more engaged volunteers, and more balanced citizens.

My wife and I enjoy the movie *Evan Almighty,* a playful recasting of the biblical story of Noah set in modern-day Washington, D.C. In the film, Congressman Evan Baxter, played by Steve Carell, is struggling with work and family balance as well as family unity. The character of God, played by Morgan Freeman, comes to Baxter and tells him to spend less time at work and instead to build an ark.[23] At first, his wife is less than convinced that this is a good idea, and the process of building the ark nearly pulls Evan's family apart. However, the opportunities God gives Evan's family to trust each other along the journey pulls them together and ensures the family unity they had hoped for. At one point God offers this explanation to Evan's wife: "If someone prays for patience, you think God gives them patience? Or does God give them the opportunity to be patient? If a person prays for courage, does God give the person courage or does God give the person opportunities to be courageous? If someone prays for their family to be closer, do you think God zaps them with warm fuzzy feelings or does God give them opportunities to love each other?"[24] There is wisdom in this observation. It is up to us to make the most of the opportunities we have to develop healthy habits.

Let me share ten practices that have made a difference for me:

1. **Begin each day with a centering phrase.**
   I have found that saying a centering phrase over and over first thing in the morning helps me begin the day with centeredness and balance. Some mornings I wake up feeling stressed and pressed. Maybe I went to bed the night before feeling anxious, or I was awakened by the children several times during the night, or I had a bad dream. But if I say my phrase over in my mind several times before I get out of bed in the morning, my head feels much clearer, and I feel more positive and less anxious.

   I most often like to begin with Psalm 118:24: "This is the day that the Lord has made; let us rejoice and be glad in it." These words take my mind off of my problems and help me think first about God. That, in turn, helps remind me of the big picture—that the world does not revolve around me. It helps me remember that even if I had a rough time the day before, today is a new day, one God has created with new opportunities. You might prefer something like, "Here I am, send me," or the *shema*—"The Lord your God, the Lord is one." Or perhaps you might try Psalm 23, the Lord's Prayer, the Doxology, or the Gloria Patria. Find something that works for you.

2. **Pray daily.**
   When you are frustrated with balance issues, pray. When you are upset at your work situation or boss, pray. When you are frustrated with your kids, pray. Prayer is a critical practice when it comes to work-life balance. It is the original, calming practice that Jesus taught and that connects us to God. C. S. Lewis is often quoted as having said, "I pray not because it changes God but because it changes me." Prayer calms, refocuses, and provides the spiritual strength we need to find balance in our days. When we pray, we tap into supernatural power. As Christians, we do not pray on

our own. We end prayers with "In Jesus' name we pray"—
because we are offering the prayer in the spirit and authority
of Jesus, our great intercessor and mediator before God.

The Lord's Prayer is a good model for prayer; in fact,
Jesus offered that prayer when the disciples asked, "Teach
us how to pray." But there is no one right way to pray.
Find what works for you. Some use the A.C.T.S. formula
(Adoration, Confession, Thanksgiving, and Supplication).
Try adoration—"Almighty God, you care about us deeply;"
Confession—"Creator God, I confess I have not loved my
neighbors as I have loved myself;" Thanksgiving—"We are
thankful that you love us;" and Supplication—"I pray for
health and for peace." Perhaps end with, "In Jesus' name we
pray. Amen."

3. **Care for your body.**
God has given you one body for this life. Caring for it
allows you to do your work and to care for others. Eating
healthfully is important. Especially when we are traveling
or working hard, we tend not to eat so well, but our diet
contributes greatly to our health.

Exercise has great rejuvenating effects. My daily exercise
is critical to my well-being. When I am feeling stressed and
out of balance, few things can rebalance me like exercise. I
have found that deep breathing, meditation, and yoga calm
and strengthen me. We have a weekly yoga ministry at our
church and, particularly when we hold it before worship, it
helps members to be centered. I also believe that monitoring
one's breathing is important. Balance is, in part, about our
reactions to conflicts between parts of our lives. Learning to
control one's breathing as a way to center and calm oneself
can give a sense of balance within pressured situations.

4. **Simplify your life.**
Leonardo Da Vinci reportedly noted, "Simplicity is the
ultimate sophistication." Edwin Way Teale is alleged to
have said, "Reduce the complexities of life by eliminating

the needless wants of life, and the labors of life reduce themselves." Jesus and his disciples lived simply. Read Mark 6:6-9:

> Then he went about among the villages teaching. He called the twelve and began to send them out two by two, and gave them authority over the unclean spirits. He ordered them to take nothing for their journey except a staff; no bread, no bag, no money in their belts; but to wear sandals and not to put on two tunics.

Jesus had access to all the riches of heaven but chose to live simply and called on his disciples to do the same. Figure out what is most important to you in life and hold on to it dearly. Let the rest go.

5. **Come to terms with your relationship with money.**
   Our desire to accumulate and spend can spur us to work extreme hours in order to make more money. We must develop a habit of budgeting our money and living within our means. We can easily get caught up in the culture of consumption to the point where we feel we must work as much as possible in order to afford the lifestyle we think we want. Clearly, working for money is necessary and important for most of us. However, I have found books like *Your Money or Your Life* by Vicki Robin, Joe Dominguez, and Monique Tilford to be helpful in my seeking to develop a healthy relationship with money.[25] If we can appreciate the need for and benefits of money while watching our expenses and not allowing the desire to make money to become our dominant value, then we can more easily make the choice to spend our time on activities other than work.

6. **Designate a quiet space in your home for rest.**
   It is important to have a space in your home to which you can retreat when feeling pressed. This is particularly essential when your family includes young children and the house can become loud. The space doesn't have to be large, but it does need to be a sanctuary for you.

7. **Invite the Holy Spirit into each activity.**

We are at our best when we invite God's Spirit into each activity of our lives. Many Africans and Native Americans I know attend to their spirituality throughout the activities of their lives. The Lakota Sioux Indians have a saying that makes the point, "Let everything you do be your religion. Let everything you say be your prayer."[26] I have a friend who has helped me think of my work and family lives as more integrated with my spiritual life. She has encouraged me to think of parenting as a spiritual time, not as a distraction. That way, each movement of my parenting can be a spiritual experience. Thinking of the routines of life as spiritual practices can make these moments sacred and can allow us to be more fully present with children and spouses, rather than viewing routines like child care as obligations one has to get through.

8. **Go on retreats and vacations.**

Rest is important enough that we should also set aside significant periods of time dedicated to it. Our bodies, minds, and spirits need to lie fallow, like farmland, in order to be refreshed. Taking a week or two of vacation can help do that. However, 43 percent of Americans do not even take all their vacation days.[27] Those are important opportunities for rest, and we should make the most of them.

Whenever I go on retreats, long weekends, or weeks away, I come back with new ideas that change my life. Just being away from the normal routine helps one see things differently. When I have a chance to listen to helpful speakers, I discover new connections and hear new perspectives, and it makes the time away transformative. I spent one summer in upstate New York at a Christian conference center working as an assistant to the chaplain. As part of one of our growth groups, we discussed how to increase balance by focusing on the most essential parts of life. As a result of that summer experience, one participant in that group simplified his space at home, his possessions, and his choices about how he spends his time so that he lives a more balanced life. His witness has helped me to make time away a priority in my own life.

9. **Commit to spending regular time with family and friends.**

   Having good times with family and friends can balance our work and caregiving responsibilities. Meals are important times to connect with family. Having dinner with family can be difficult for pastors and other congregational leaders who have evening meetings, so we need to find other times for fun with family and friends. Whenever possible, I try to come home for dinner before returning to church for meetings. I meet monthly with a group of men for fellowship. I participate in a monthly clergy support group. They make a great difference for me. The perspective and support we gain from relationships can make such a difference when we are stressed, overwhelmed, and trying to balance work and life.

10. **Take a break each evening before bed.**

    There is an old saying, "Don't go to bed angry." I think we should add, "Don't go to bed right after doing work." For many years I worked late into the evening after my family was asleep, sometimes past midnight. However, I got to the point where I knew I needed more sleep. After my twin girls were born, I decided to put a limit on my evening work. My grandfather used to say, "This is enough for today. That's what the good Lord made tomorrow for." I have made those words my evening mantra. This has freed me in the evening for more time with my spouse, and it has allowed me to go to sleep with a clearer mind. I have found that evenings are best for reading. Ideally, I also try to end my days with journaling and a time of prayer, meditation, or some other practice that will clear my mind. Not only do I sleep better, but when I am rested and alert, I find it's much easier to keep my days in balance.

These ten practices have made a difference for me. I am not perfect in following them, but when I stick with them I find them most helpful. Annie Dillard said, "How you spend your days is how you spend your life." If we add some healthy habits to each day of our lives, we will find that those practices and the disciplines that flow from them will bring us more balance.

For Reflection

1. Which of the practices mentioned above do you do already? What new practices will you try? What other practices help you feel balanced?
2. Finish and re-read your Act and Evaluate Your Time chart in Appendix 3. What does it tell you about yourself? Does anything surprise you? Are there any changes you would like to make after filling it out and reading it over?

CREATING A SCHEDULE THAT WORKS FOR YOU

Therefore I tell you, do not worry about your life, what you will eat or drink, or about your body, what you will wear. Is not life more than food, and the body more than clothing? Look at the birds of the air; they neither sow nor reap nor gather into barns, and yet your heavenly Father feeds them. Are you not of more value than they? And can any of you by worrying add a single hour to the span of your life? And why do you worry about clothing? Consider the lilies of the field, how they grow; they neither toil nor spin, yet I tell you, even Solomon in all his glory was not clothed like one of these. But if God so clothes the grass of the field, which is alive today and tomorrow is

thrown into the oven, will he not much more clothe you—
you of little faith? Therefore do not worry, saying, "What
will we eat?" or "What will we drink?" or "What will we
wear?" For it is the Gentiles who strive for all these things;
and indeed your heavenly Father knows that you need all
these things. But strive first for the kingdom of God and
his righteousness, and all these things will be given to you
as well. So do not worry about tomorrow, for tomorrow
will bring worries of its own.

—Matthew 6:25-34

Samuel Johnson is quoted as having said, "The chains of habit are
too weak to be felt until they are too strong to be broken."[28] I have
found that schedules help me stay balanced. At the church I try
to do my research, sermon writing, administration, Bible study,
and worship planning on the same days each week. This allows
me to avoid the tyranny of the urgency that comes with having to
scramble to write a sermon at the end of the week. Then, as I have
mentioned, I also try to read Scripture, pray, exercise, and write in
my journal at the same times each day.

If we don't have schedules for ourselves, we are always reacting
to other people's requests, needs, and wants, and that can throw us
off balance. I still spend a lot of time reacting to others; but if I set
a schedule, I can, to a greater degree, set the agenda and form the
life I want. I can more easily stay centered and balanced.

Scheduling is consistent with the Reformed tradition. John
Calvin developed his own type of *lectio divina*, or sacred reading
of the Bible, as a daily spiritual exercise. Richard Baxter, one of
the great Puritans, set aside thirty minutes for daily meditation
on the word of God. John Bailey encouraged families to read the
Bible every day. The seventeenth-century Puritan Lewis Bayly
wrote *The Practice of Piety*, a guide to the daily spiritual life for the
Puritans.[29] Bayly suggested reading Scripture three times a day—
morning, noon, and night. By reading a chapter at each session,
and then the remainder on New Year's Eve, a person could finish
the whole Bible in a year. The weekly schedule in worship for many

Reformed congregations includes offering a prayer for illumination before the day's Scripture lessons are read. This prayer not only asks for God's blessing but also helps worshipers focus on the here and now so they are more present in hearing and better prepared to understand, internalize, and act on the Word of God. I recommend such a prayer before you read Scripture each day as part of your schedule as well.

Scheduling matters for both congregations and pastoral leaders. For congregations to attract new members, particularly families with children, they must take into account the scheduling needs and conflicts of potential members. Each congregation should encourage youth and adult education by developing a series of Christian formation programs for children, youth, and adults on Sunday mornings. Child care on Sunday mornings and during weekly programming can be important for families with children. For some congregations, it will make sense to hold church school during worship. For others, church school for all ages is best before or after worship. For some churches, holding a worship service at 5:00 on Sunday evenings can attract a target audience. Each congregation should prayerfully consider what is right for it, taking into account the schedules of its congregants and potential members. Churches that ignore the scheduling issues of members during the week may lose out. Churches also do well to teach the priority of worship on the Lord's Day for all members. The point is not to retreat from the importance of Sunday and the centrality of worship, but to be realistic about scheduling.

Scheduling matters for congregational leaders. I have found that following a schedule helps me live in the moment. When I am stuck in long meetings I sometimes find my mind wandering toward years past and thinking about grasses that I remember being green, whether they were or not. I might start thinking about all the "places to go, people to see, things to do" on my calendar. I know I am not alone in this, for I have talked with people whose guilt about past actions threatens to overwhelm their enjoying the present. Or they worry constantly about what they should be doing next. As the young girl sings in the musical *Annie*, "Tomorrow, tomorrow, I love you, tomorrow." Calvin called the human tendency to rush through the present "restlessness." Many times we find it easier to focus our energy on the future or to brood about the past than to face the challenges or embrace the opportunities of the present.

Yet we are at our best when we learn to live in the moment. My wife and I once traveled to the Canadian Rockies to attend a wedding. The trip was made challenging when half of our luggage never made it, and we were stuck in the hotel without luggage for a few days. There I struck up a conversation with a man who was traveling across Canada by train. He said he preferred to travel by train rather than plane, because the train allowed him to become aware of each city and province and mountain on the way. It takes longer, the man said, but such a journey works if you can resist asking every ten minutes, "Are we there yet?" He said, "If you can go without asking that question, you will have an enjoyable ride." Many of us travel through life asking, "Are we there yet?" We aren't always sure where we are going, but we seem to be in a hurry to get there.

Depending on our life situation, we may not have the kind of control over our time that allows setting a daily schedule with precision. However, all of us have some degree of control over our days, at least over our free time. If we are disciplined about how we use our free time, this can allow space for rest and appropriate spiritual practices. Furthermore, as I speak with employers and employer groups, I find that they are, perhaps surprisingly, open to employee input about how time is allocated during the workday. Finally, as noted and as we'll discuss in the next chapter, the movement towards more workforce flexibility in the United States has potential to allow us more ability to develop daily schedules that work for both employers and employees. Workers usually become more productive as a result of having more input. Congregations and individuals can and should work to promote workplace flexibility.

We live in a pressured world where focusing on the present can be difficult, but ordering our time can enable us to be more present in each moment. This is where prioritization can be helpful. Try asking, "What are the most important activities for me today?" Pick a limited, achievable number and write them down. I usually limit my daily list to three major priorities. I try to make sure at least one item on my list provides spiritual refreshment to me. Then I decide how much time I want to set aside for each one. I realize life is full of interruptions, but I have found it helpful to set a general plan for how I will use my time each day. This schedule frees me to live in the moment within the structure of that time plan, not worrying about getting everything done or what comes next. It allows me to be disciplined with my time, so I am able to complete the three items on my daily to-do list.

I have also found it helpful to have some external mechanism to help guard and support my use of time. I sometimes share with a coworker how long I am supposed to be in a meeting and then that person calls when the time is up, so I don't have to worry about the time during the meeting. Or I set an alarm when I begin a meditation time, so I don't worry that I will go so long in my spiritual practice that it bleeds over into other parts of the day. I can then focus fully on the prayer. I also use such mechanisms to limit how long I work on a project before taking a break.

Knowing that someone or something will alert me when the time I have set aside for a particular task has ended enables me to focus on the content of each activity instead of on its duration. It allows me to be more fully present to that person or activity rather than thinking about what has happened or what is coming next. This allows me to enjoy the content of what I'm working on and, ultimately, to balance my work and caregiving responsibilities with times of rejuvenation. Ordering my time by setting a schedule ensures I get the rest I need, that I fulfill my responsibilities to work and family, and in the end, that I live with balance.

If we view our time as connected to God, then we should take seriously how we use our time. If time is holy, we should be intentional about stewarding the gift of time, just as we steward our financial resources. Remembering that the way I use my time is part of my stewardship of the gifts God has given me helps me maintain this balance.

I have found it helpful to think about time as being both cyclical and seasonal, and to develop cyclical patterns, practices, and rituals each day. For values to become habits, we must repeat them. I have found success in organizing my spiritual practices around the cycle of the day as well. But I must confess that I don't always succeed in following my schedule. There are days when my aspirations exceed my ability to fulfill each of my practices. I am regular with my morning mantra, my midday prayer, my afternoon exercise, and my evening prayers, although sometimes my noon and evening prayers happen more quickly than I'd like. The midday prayer may be at my desk, and the evening prayer in bed; but I still find the habit to be important. I am pretty faithful with my journaling, though I sometimes end up journaling at times other than evening, even though I find reflection and journaling in the evening tends to be the most beneficial. Currently, I struggle most with reading Scripture consistently each morning. My children are my alarm clock, and then life takes over. I read Scripture each week in staff meetings, Bible studies, and sermon preparation, but when I am able to read Scripture devotionally in the morning, it does make a difference.

Don't worry if you don't fulfill all your goals or keep your schedule perfectly each and every day. None of us is perfect. If you are reading this, you likely have pressures on your time that make following your schedule difficult each day. Be flexible. Be practical. Be realistic. Be committed. Set a schedule and do your best. Let me offer an example of the kind of daily schedule I have found most helpful.

Morning

I begin with my mantra and then I try to do some meditative Scripture reading whenever possible. I enjoy reading one or two

Bible passages over and over again at least five times. I particularly enjoy the Book of Psalms. I often use the PCUSA daily lectionary and have tried at times to put a brief comment on the passage on my blog. I try to begin the day with Scripture because putting on the ideas of faith can be a good way to start the day. The will of God, not our will, should set our priorities at the beginning of the day. Focusing on Scripture—meditating on God's presence in the text, contemplating God, and then opening our hearts so God speaks to us—can make a real difference. Read the passage over and over and contemplate what it means. Then let it guide you during the morning.

Noon

I have found that prayer at noon is important. Calvin wrote, ". . . unless we fix certain hours in the day for prayer, it easily slips from our memory."[30] The act of meditation—opening oneself to God and resting—lowers one's stress in the middle of the day. Through prayer we can have conversations with God that will shape the rest of our day. I try to pray for fifteen or twenty minutes in the middle of each day. Even ten minutes of quiet prayer in the middle of a busy day can calm us, connect us with God, and help us establish balance.

If you cannot carve out that much time, try eight and one-half minutes of prayer at noon. God modeled weekly Sabbath by taking one day out of each seven-day week for rest; perhaps our daily prayer time might consist of one-seventh of an hour, or about eight and one-half minutes. Would you be able to pray for about eight and one-half minutes each noon? It takes time to calm oneself and to enter deeply into a prayerful mindset. My midday practice often prevents my lunch hour from being as social as I would like it to be, but I find it is a helpful spiritual time.

Each week, friends and parishioners ask me to pray for them. I make a list of those phone, e-mail, and in-person requests and pray for the people and situations on the list at noon. We also send out a weekly e-mail to church members that lists significant needs in the congregation so people can support one another in prayer. That list is another helpful guide for my noon intercessory prayers.

Prayer can be an effective way to separate ourselves from the constant demands of life, to help us calm down, to provide some spiritual rest in the middle of each day, and to provide some balance within our work lives. Find what works for you during the day. Find a quiet place. Meditate or pray. Just being quiet during the day may be helpful to you. Make it an important habit in the middle of your day.

Mid-afternoon

I try to exercise each afternoon. The meditative qualities of exercise make it a spiritual time for me. Even on days when working out doesn't feel particularly "spiritual," I find that getting my heart moving really helps my sense of balance anyway. Exercise is good for my health and offers me a break from work. It rejuvenates me, and it sets me on a good path for continuing my day. I enjoy swimming, tennis, using an elliptical machine and ergometer (rowing machine), walking the dog, lifting light weights, and doing sit-ups and pushups. I try to do some combination of these for thirty minutes each afternoon. I have also found at times that reading about faith, the Bible, and spiritual formation and practice, and then writing my thoughts about God can be a helpful and important afternoon practice.

Evening

I try to allow quiet time for reflection each evening. Again, this is a challenge in a family with young children. Much as I begin the day by "inhaling" through Scripture, I try to "exhale" at the end of the day with reflection. I try to write down what I learned during the day, quotes or a story I heard, words of wisdom, and things to think about for other days. I try to be positive at the end of the day before I go to sleep. Reflecting at the end of the day, perhaps through writing in a journal, can help us understand ourselves better and better know our limits. Reflection can help us see how and where to improve the balance of our lives. Many of the early Reformers kept journals of God's actions and providences each day. Keep a journal by your bedside and use it each night for reflection.

I often borrow one model for evening reflection from St. Ignatius' meditations. Inspired by and building on the ideas of Ignatius, let me offer some steps for evening reflection and journal writing:

1. **Review the day.** Allow your consciousness to flow freely and bring forth memories of the day. Write them down.
2. **Recognize the presence of God.** In an Ignatian prayer, a candle is often lit or a moment of silence observed.
3. **Remember God's gifts.** Write down something from the day for which you are grateful.
4. **Reconcile with God.** As you review your day, you may come face to face with some of your weaknesses and short-comings. Ask for forgiveness. Make notes in your journal about how you will extend forgiveness to others.
5. **Resolve to make changes.** As you begin to think about the next day, make resolutions about what to do differently.
6. **Make use of a journal.** Write about your use of time, your sense of work-life balance, the activities that either brought you joy and balance or sapped your energy and wasted your time, and about your general walk with God. I sometimes also write poetry in my journal, which I find opens me to a creative spirit. Put a Bible and a pad of paper by your bed for journaling. Don't worry about perfection in journaling; just get down the ideas. My handwriting is terrible, but I still write a lot of notes in my journal.
7. **Retire focusing on God.** Close with prayer to give thanks and to ask for a good sleep. I believe the last thing we should do at night is to read a brief passage of Scripture and pray,

so that the last thing we think about before our subconscious goes to work while we sleep is a positive idea that comes from God. Reflecting on ourselves in the evening can be helpful, but it's best to end the day thinking about something other than ourselves. We should end the day where we began, by thinking about God. My last prayer is between me and God. It's personal and ends the day with a focus on the Almighty, so my spirit connects with the holy. St. Benedict instructed his monks to recite Psalm 4:8 each night, "In peace will I both lie down and sleep, for you alone, O Lord, make me to dwell in safety."[31] Not a bad way to end a day.

Whatever order works for you, develop a daily spiritual schedule. Write it down and follow it. It can help you live in the moment and can help turn values into disciplines, disciplines into habits, and habits into healthy, balanced living.

For Reflection

1. Do you have a daily spiritual schedule? If not, what sort of schedule might work for you?
2. What spiritual practices help you separate from the patterns of the world?
3. For five consecutive days, try to set aside time for Scripture reading each morning, for prayer at noon, for exercise in the afternoon, and for self-reflection by writing in a journal in the evening. At the end of the five days, consider how you feel about the experience. Do you feel more in balance? Do you feel more productive when you return to work as a result? Do you feel like continuing these practices, or are you glad you are finished? Do you want to continue keeping a spiritual schedule? If so, what will you now commit to doing?
4. Try the same pattern for a longer period of time, perhaps adding some spiritual reading and writing. How do you find this experience?

CHAPTER 6

We Need to Change Our Societal Structures

Moses's father-in-law said to him, "What you are doing is not good. You will surely wear yourself out, both you and these people with you. For the task is too heavy for you; you cannot do it alone. Now listen to me. I will give you counsel, and God be with you . . . You should also look for able men among all the people, men who fear God, are trustworthy, and hate dishonest gain . . . So it will be easier for you, and they will bear the burden with you. If you do this, and God so commands you, then you will be able to endure, and all these people will go to their home in peace.

Exodus 18: 17–23

Pastors are called to care not only about the members of their congregations, but also about the state of our nation and world. Many churches affirm this principle and are involved in some sort of mission or outreach. I believe congregations should also consider how to improve the conditions in society that affect people's work-life balance for the benefit of people everywhere. As we have seen, work-life imbalance is a significant challenge for millions of Americans both inside and outside the church. The structures of our society affect how well individuals balance work and life.

In this chapter we'll look first at the call for congregations to care about the conditions of the world. Second, we'll examine how workplace flexibility can help address work-life imbalance. Third, we'll look at some specific policies that could make a difference. Throughout, we'll seek to discover how congregational leaders can get involved.

CARING ABOUT THE CONDITIONS OF THE WORLD

> We make a living by what we earn; we make a life by what we give.
>
> —Winston Churchill

Christ calls us to care about the world. Christian missionaries have long traveled the world to spread the Gospel, and Christian service programs have, for many years, reached out globally to help those in need. Chances are that your congregation is involved in some mission outreach. By influencing public policy and changing the structures of society at large, congregations can help many more people than they could just by ministering to people in their local area. That is why the churches throughout the years have been involved with public policies on any number of issues, from slavery and civil rights to defending life, foreign aid, and economic growth and justice.

We read in Mark 12:28-31 about a time when Jesus was asked about the greatest commandment of God:

> One of the scribes came near and heard them disputing with one another, and seeing that he answered them well, he asked him, "Which commandment is the first of all?" Jesus answered, "The first is, 'Hear, O Israel: the Lord our God, the Lord is one;

and you shall love the Lord your God with all your heart, and with all your soul, and with all your mind, and with all your strength.' The second is this, 'You shall love your neighbor as yourself.' There is no other commandment greater than these."

All who seek to love God must also seek to love their neighbors. In 1 John 4, we read that if we cannot love our brothers and sisters, we cannot say we love God. Love of God and love of neighbor are inextricably bound together.

What does it mean to love our neighbors? In Luke 10, a lawyer asked Jesus what he must do to inherit eternal life. Jesus answered with words similar to those in the passage above: "You shall love your God with all your heart, soul, mind, and strength and your neighbor as yourself." The lawyer then asked Jesus, "Who is my neighbor?" Jesus responded by telling the well-known Parable of the Good Samaritan. The Samaritan comes upon a man who has been mugged, beaten, and left for dead. Other people have walked past, ignoring the man and his need, but the Samaritan stops and, out of compassion, helps the man, a complete stranger, to safety. Given the state of Jewish-Samaritan relations and the dangerous conditions along the road to Jericho, it was a risk for the Samaritan to stop.

This story is familiar to many of us, and it underscores that we all are called to care about the world—even people who are strangers to us, those whom we do not know. We demonstrate our commitment to God as we help others around us. If we are to love people, including those we do not know—and even our enemies—we must work to improve the structures of society that affect all of us.

Many congregations are involved in mission because they believe that they can make a difference in the world for others. If congregational leaders believe that work-life balance is an important subject, we should care about the structures of society, including public policy, that affect the work-life balance of not only their congregants but of everyone.

For Reflection

1. In what ways do you show you care for people whom you do not know personally?
2. Reread the Good Samaritan story. How does it affect your view of caring for people outside your church or who are different from you?
3. In what ways is the church called to care about the structures of society?
4. Is work-life balance an issue you believe the church should be involved in addressing? If so, how should it be involved?

WHY WORKPLACE FLEXIBILITY MATTERS TO A BALANCED LIFE

Semper Gumby: Always flexible.

—Anonymous

Flexibility matters for anyone trying to balance work and family. Many of us experience so many unexpected interruptions that we must be flexible in our schedules to stay sane and centered and successfully maintain our balance. Yet it can be very difficult for many of us to find flexibility within our work. If work-life balance becomes a priority for congregational leaders themselves, the next step is for the church to share the ideas broadly with the world. Work-life imbalance is not just a personal issue. It is a public problem that, as we have seen, leads to poor work performance, health issues, relationship stress, lower national economic competitiveness, reduced family time, and decreased happiness for too many people.[1]

According to Stephen Wing of Corporate Voices for Working Families:

Today, business leaders, working mothers and fathers, advocates, community leaders, and local, state, and federal officials
understand that our ability as a nation to harness the talent of
our workforce to be globally competitive depends on family-
friendly practices that help all workers manage both work and
life.[2]

While the nature of the American family has changed a great deal
over the past generation or two, the structure of work in America
has not kept pace. As has been mentioned, most U.S. families now
have two breadwinners. Technology and globalization are major
factors. Yet most jobs are still structured around set locations and
hours, most U.S. labor laws were written in the 1930s, and most
career paths still begin in one's early twenties and continue until
one is over sixty, with significant costs for workers who take time
off for family.

Work-life conflict is shaped not only by the total time spent on
the job, but also by the degree of flexibility and control a worker
has over the hours worked. The ability to have more flexibility
and control over how and when we work can help relieve some
of the pressures of work-life imbalance. Work-life balance is, in
many ways, about reducing conflicts between the work we need
to get done to earn our incomes and care for our families and the
life we want to enjoy. Increasing flexibility can benefit employers,
employees, families, and communities. It can help families feel less
stressed and can help employers maintain a more engaged and
committed workforce. A recent survey by WorldatWork found
that part-time schedules, flextime, teleworking, and other forms of
workplace flexibility increase employee motivation, engagement,
and satisfaction, and lower employee turnover.[3]

Such practices can help both businesses and churches attract
talent, retain valued employees, increase morale and job satisfaction, and improve staff productivity. Many organizations that
provide work-life or flexibility programs find that employees
who take advantage of these programs are less "burned out" than

those who don't. According to Kathleen Christensen of the Alfred P. Sloan Foundation, workplace flexibility is now a critical need because "workers are exhausted, and they are fed up with having to choose between work and family. Businesses of all sizes have proven that flexible workplaces are the most effective workplaces."[4]

Workplace Flexibility 2010, a non-profit educational group based at Georgetown Law School, has defined three forms of flexibility in work that I think are helpful.[5] First, they describe *Flexible Work Arrangements* (FWAs):

> [FWAs] alter the time and/or place that work is conducted on a regular basis—in a manner that is as manageable and predictable as possible for both employees and employers. FWAs provide: flexibility in the scheduling of hours worked, such as alternative work schedules (e.g., non-traditional start and end times, flex time, or compressed workweeks) and arrangements regarding overtime, predictable scheduling, and shift and break schedules; flexibility in the amount of hours worked, such as part time work, job shares, phased retirement or part year work; and flexibility in the place of work, such as working at home, at a satellite location or at different locations.

For example, flexible work arrangements might mean the start and end times of the workday differ from the traditional 8:00 a.m. to 5:00 p.m. times, while the same number of hours per day is maintained. Or, an employee might be able to work from home or vary the starting times of the workday over the course of the week. One might also work a compressed workweek, working longer one week in exchange for shorter days or a day off during another week.[6]

The second type of flexibility the group identified is *Time Off*, which "provides leave from work for a defined period of time to address unexpected or ongoing personal and family needs." There are three types of time off:

- Short-Term Time Off (STO) is used to address the ordinary predictable and unpredictable needs of life (e.g., a sick employee, a sick child, a child's school conference, a death in the family, a home repair).

- Episodic Time Off (EPTO) is used to address a recurring predictable need for time off from work (e.g., an employee who has—or cares for a family member who has—an illness or chronic health condition that flares up sporadically, an employee who volunteers regularly in the community, an employee who is obtaining advanced training).

- Extended Time Off (EXTO) is used to address a need for time off from work for a single reason that extends for more than five days but less than one year (e.g., caring for a newborn or newly adopted child, having a serious health condition or caring for a family member with a serious health condition, or serving in the military).[7]

The third category identified is *Career Flexibility*. Career flexibility recognizes that careers in the twenty-first-century economy often follow cyclical progressions rather than linear ones. Out of necessity or personal choice, individuals may leave the workforce for a period of time but will need or want to reenter the workforce at a later point in time. For example, some workers may leave the workforce at certain points in order to further their education. Others might leave in order to meet family and caregiving responsibilities. There are three critical components that make up career flexibility. The first is career exit—the point in time when an individual decides to leave the workforce. The second is career maintenance—the period of time spent out of the workforce by an individual. The third is career reentry—the point in time when an individual chooses to get back into the workforce.[8]

These definitions might seem like "policy wonk" talk, but workplace flexibility is a very practical issue and one to which I believe church leaders can relate to. Much of congregational life requires its leaders, particularly pastors, to be flexible. Pastors must deal with unpredictable pastoral care needs and other emergencies. Members often want to meet at times when they won't have to take off from work—which often means after 5:00 p.m. or on weekends. Funerals, weddings, counseling sessions, and meetings can occur in the evenings or on weekends. To meet such challenges, a pastor's work schedule must be somewhat flexible. Many pastors have flexible work arrangements within days, work evenings, and weekends. In addition, as the number of women in ministry has increased, churches find that more and more clergy seek to take time away from work to have children or care for family, and then return to service in the church.

As many Christian leaders have become more involved in interfaith dialogue, they can become interested in flexibility to support religious observances. I once moderated an interfaith briefing at the U.S. House of Representatives on the nexus between personal faith and work-life balance policy. The Christian, Jewish, and Muslim leaders at this briefing all agreed that work-life balance is a serious issue that needs to be addressed in their communities.[9] The Jewish and Muslim clergy were particularly concerned about people having flexibility for religious observance. For many Muslims, being able to attend prayers on Fridays is critical; for many Jews, participation in high holy days is important, even when those days conflict with work. The leaders from all traditions shared the deep need they saw for their congregants to achieve more balance. They also shared a hope that both faith leaders and public policy leaders could work to increase the flexibility of U.S. workplaces to help make that possible.

Based on my own experience, research, and personal discussions, I have found that one of the greatest factors in successfully balancing work and life is flexibility. Moreover, in the private sector, businesses are increasingly offering workplace flexibility as a management strategy and tool. Many employers recognize that flexible work arrangements allow them to recruit and retain the best workers.[10] For example, Jet Blue, PNC Bank, Kraft Food, Wachovia, J.C. Penney, and HEB Grocery Company have all acknowledged the benefits of offering flexibility to their employees. I have heard some business people say that in the future there will be two kinds of companies—"the flexible and the dead."

Flexibility makes my life more balanced. Being able to go home to help care for my children has been key to making my life work. I have been able to pick up my son from nursery school, attend doctor's appointments with my wife, and go to the gym to exercise. I took some paternity leave after the birth of our twins. Having that extended time off was critical. I did not have such flexibility during my years working for the government, so I understand that many people do not have flexible options. Furthermore, I recognize that not all types of flexibility work in all jobs. For example, it would be difficult for a security guard to telecommute. However, many jobs could be made more flexible than they are currently.

I think church leaders should look for ways to become involved in national discussions about workplace flexibility and policy changes. They could encourage church members to seek out employers that offer flexibility and to speak with their current employers about work-life challenges they face. Many employers would grant a flexible schedule if employees would ask for one. If you are an employer or a leader of a congregation or other organization, ensure that those who work for your organization enjoy as much flexibility as possible, consistent with the needs of the organization. I have found that managing my team in a results-focused workplace and giving my colleagues flexibility helps everyone be more productive.

For Reflection

1. How flexible is your work situation?
2. How flexible is work for the staff of your church?
3. How can you use flexibility to improve your work-life balance?
4. How can your congregation encourage members who are employers to support the work-life balance of their employees?
5. Can your congregation encourage more workplace flexibility in U.S. public policy? If so, how?

How Societal Structures Could Be Changed

I don't roll on Shabbos!
—Fictional bowler Walter Sobchak, explaining his
refusal to compete on the Sabbath, *The Big Lebowski*
(Polygram, 1998)

I once moderated a panel discussion at the New America Foundation entitled, "How Expanding Flexibility in the Workplace Supports Religious Americans." The participants included representatives from Georgetown Law School, the American Jewish Committee, the Union of Orthodox Jewish Congregations of America, President Obama's faith-based advisory board, the Sikh Coalition, the General Conference of Seventh-Day Adventists, and the American Islamic Congress. The participants spoke of how flexibility can help religious Americans in our nation's increasingly diverse workforce. They stressed that policy changes to our society's structures could make a difference, not only for religious observance, but for the work-life balance of all.

There are a variety of policy areas in which individuals or congregations could get involved to make a difference. Each congregation needs to look at its own strengths and interests, its own geography and resources of time and energy, to determine which method of becoming involved in advancing workplace flexibility in society is right for it. Yet if we believe Christians are called to love their neighbors, that millions of Americans are suffering from work-life imbalance, and that there are policy solutions that could address the issue, then congregations have an opportunity to become involved with workplace flexibility policy to transform the world.

Our state and federal representatives have the ability under a variety of laws—including the Fair Labor Standards Act and the Family and Medical Leave Act—to make changes that can encourage workplace flexibility. Obviously, most congregations are not equipped to develop sophisticated advocacy arms on legislative issues. However, individual members can encourage change in their own workplaces by discussing flexibility with their employers or by advocating individually. As with poverty, environmental conservation, and peacemaking, congregations can pass resolutions in favor of legislation and encourage their denominational bodies to do so, can write letters to their state and federal representatives encouraging family-friendly public policies, can join together across denominations to visit Capitol Hill to ask for policies that encourage workplace flexibility, and can work through their national outreach and public witness officers to include work-life balance among their areas of focus.

Let me suggest several policy ideas congregational leaders might consider addressing to advocate for greater flexibility and work-life balance.[11]

1. **Promoting Telework.**

   Telework enables employees to use technology to work remotely rather than making a daily commute, thus increasing flexibility in the location and hours of work. Telework has many advantages: It can cut driving times, decrease pollution, reduce demand for gasoline, make it easier for people with disabilities to contribute in the marketplace, and help support businesses in case of a natural disaster or terrorist attack by dispersing the workforce. According to Kathryn Fonner of the University of Wisconsin–Milwaukee, telework can reduce stress. She found that employees who telework at least three days a week reported decreased work-life conflict.[12] Employees working remotely are, on average, shielded from many of the stressful aspects of the workplace. Sun Microsystems has an "open work" policy that empowers employees to "work effectively, virtually anywhere." Telework is widely acknowledged to have significant benefits for both employers and employees, yet only about 15 percent of employees nationally telework even one day per week. There are a variety of policies the federal government can pursue to encourage telework.

- The Department of Labor could provide online information about best practices for telework and descriptions of the technology and procedures necessary to enable widespread telework.
- Just as the development of the interstate highway system in the 1950s transformed commerce by allowing products to be moved more extensively, broadband technology could be expanded to link people more fully. One strategy would be to install fiber-optic cable whenever highways are torn up for repair.
- Tax incentives could be given to companies and employees who purchase equipment needed for telework.
- Clarifying the tax treatment of telework could help as well. Because of differing state taxing systems, some teleworkers may pay income tax both in the state where they live and the one where they work. Because the law is ambiguous, the government could clarify to encourage taxation by only one jurisdiction.

2. **Supporting phased retirement.**
   Older workers, many of whom have seen their retirement savings slashed by the 2008 economic crisis, often have a desire and a need to continue working but want to do so in a more flexible way than they have in the past. They should be able to receive a portion of their retirement savings while also maintaining a working relationship with their employer. Currently, employers who wish to develop phased retirement programs may face legal obstacles under the Employee Retirement Income Security Act (ERISA) and the Internal Revenue Code (Tax Code), which may restrict employees in receiving distributions from their pensions until they have fully severed employment or have reached a certain age. This prevents individuals from partially retiring

and working reduced hours while receiving a portion of their pension benefit to supplement their reduced income. The law could be adjusted to allow older workers to continue to work while beginning to draw down some of their retirement savings.

3. **Promoting quality child care.**

   In the United States, some 11 million children under five are in some kind of child-care arrangement each day. Millions of other, older children are involved as well. For working parents, few issues are more important than the care one's children receive during the workday. Parents want their children to be in high quality settings with good instructors so the parents can go to work while the children have opportunities to learn and grow. Yet, child care is expensive. From a policy standpoint, promoting accessibility, affordability, and quality in U.S. child care systems can help promote work-life balance for American families.

4. **Revising the Fair Labor Standards Act.**

   One change to promote workplace flexibility would be to amend the Fair Labor Standards Act (FLSA) to allow workers to labor up to fifty hours in a given week without triggering overtime (up from forty hours), but no more than eighty hours in a two-week period. Currently, an employee who is not exempt from overtime pay cannot work more than forty hours in a week without the employer having to pay overtime. Yet, some hourly workers would prefer to work fifty hours one week and only thirty the next in order to spend more time with their family that second week. I also have colleagues who want to take their overtime hours as compensatory time, and the FLSA should be revised to allow that.

5. **Clearing up misconceptions about the law.**

   Many employers are reluctant to offer flexible work arrangements because they have misperceptions about the law. For example, some employers believe that hourly workers cannot work a compressed workweek of four ten-hour days without the business incurring overtime liability. However, such a schedule is allowed. The U.S. Department of Labor should help clarify that such creative examples of workplace flexibility are already available under current law.

6. **Supporting career flexibility.**

Technology is developing each day to allow more and more people to learn remotely. Lifelong learning opportunities should be encouraged to allow workers to maintain and develop their skills, especially if they need or choose to take some time away from the workforce.

7. **Encouraging conversations about flexibility between employers and employees.**

Employers have told me that if their employees asked for flexibility, they would try to grant the requests in most cases. Great Britain enacted a law in 2004 that gave employees the right to request a flexible schedule. However, similar "right to request" legislation has gone nowhere in the United States, in no small part because most proposals contain provisions that seek to enforce a solution when employers and employees disagree. The development of similar legislation in Australia that allows an employer to deny a request for legitimate business reasons might provide a starting point for a bipartisan conversation about a model that could be considered in the United States.

8. **Considering work sharing.**

The economic downturn that began in 2008 has potential to highlight bipartisan work-life balance policies. The Fair Labor Standards Act and its forty-hour workweek became law in the Depression-era as an effort to promote work sharing and thus reduce unemployment. In a similar way today, rather than laying off workers (leaving them with no job or work to balance), employers could be encouraged to reduce workers' hours, which would allow more workers to remain part of the workforce. Rather than the government disbursing money to persons who have been laid off in the form of unemployment benefits, those same funds could help supplement the salaries of employees who work reduced hours. For many people, being unemployed is extremely stressful and does not allow a sense of balance, even though a person has lots of non-work time. Work sharing might allow someone who has been working hard to work fewer hours and be more balanced while still maintaining his or her attachment to work. Such a solution could provide an ongoing salary, rather than a pink slip, as well as opportunities for an employee to have more time for family.

9. **Developing award programs to promote flexibility.**
   The government might provide recognition to organizations that provide flexible work arrangements.

10. **Promoting access to government information.**
    Employers have told me they are hungry for information on how to implement flexibility and support their employees in achieving work-life balance. Many have expressed interest in attending trainings, receiving technical assistance, and being able to access a "one-stop clearinghouse" of information. The government could provide training and technical assistance to both employers and employees on how to effectively implement flexibility policies and programs. This support could include regional conferences, on-site training, webinars, conference calls, and distance-learning courses.

Church leaders should seek to educate their members about work-life balance and possible solutions such as workplace flexibility as a starting point to begin to advocate for changes in the world. Of course, congregations are not going to suddenly change American workplaces by themselves. However, as people and institutions called to be involved with caring about and transforming the world, we must begin getting involved in changing public policies and start moving our culture toward a greater appreciation of the importance of balance. These are just some of the ways that congregational leaders, individually or collectively, could be involved in promoting work-life balance and workplace flexibility in our nation.

For Reflection

1. What does workplace flexibility mean to you?
2. How could you inspire your congregation to be more involved in fostering work-life balance in your community and nationally?
3. How can you become involved in public policies that change the structures of society to encourage work-life balance?

Epilogue

Maybe the human race isn't a race after all.
—Wally, *The Switch* (Miramax, 2010)

Work-life balance is a daily journey. It is not a destination. Because each day is unpredictable and the pressures we face today may be different from those of the day before, we must constantly renew our efforts to achieve balance. It takes commitment and work. Planning is critical, but many unexpected things will happen each day. I have found that my progress is usually two steps forward and one step back. Yet, church leaders can make progress in work-life balance that contributes to their happiness and that of their congregations. When congregational leaders are balanced, they are more effective.

I was able to develop and test my own disciplines as I wrote this book. The process of writing the book has helped me to crystallize and better follow ideas I know are important but too often have been inconsistent in executing. I began putting this project together based on a class I had taught using some graduate school research. When I started writing the book, we had a four-year-old and a two-year-old—and then our twins arrived. Having four children under five at home while working full-time allowed me to test my principles in the face of a lot of work-life conflict. My life, like that of many parents—especially those with young children—is quite fragmented. I have a hard time getting uninterrupted space to focus on work projects. But congregational leaders are always pulled in a lot of directions. Pastors often have to be managers, performers, counselors, facilities administrators, staff organizers, and teachers, to name just a few of the hats we must wear. Lay leaders have their own families and careers on top of the significant amounts of time many invest in the lives of their congregations. My experience of writing taught me the importance of discipline, of setting and keeping a schedule as much as possible, and of how workplace flexibility supports work-life balance.

A few months after the births of our twins, my wife and I went to New York City for a brief getaway. At the time my wife had not spent any extended amount of time away from our then two-and-a-half-year-old, let alone our infant twins. The demands of parenthood were so significant that it took going to the busiest city in the country for us to find peace. Our hotel had a roof-deck restaurant. Just sitting there for an evening having dinner was such a special break from our routine. The meal was fine, but the moment was to savor. A pianist provided great background music. There was a brief rainstorm, but we didn't care. We had the Queensboro Bridge behind us. At first, the traffic seemed loud, but the noise became a nice background hum that we found almost soothing. No children, just us. No crying, just talking. No diapers, just dinner. We shared stories about life before kids and made plans for life after they grow up. The time together was exactly what we needed. It was God-filled time. It was sacred time of rest that briefly provided balance in our otherwise crazy lives.

I believe I am making progress toward the work-life balance I desire. I hope you are, too. I try neither to idolize my work nor to be idle. I am getting better at recognizing the role religion plays in my own moments of imbalance and how it can help me live with more balance. We are not meant to do nothing; at the same time, we are not meant to try to do everything. We are to use God's gifts and to follow God's calls. God gives us only so many breaths to take, and they can't all be full of work. We must seek balance.

We must be willing to steward our time for God and to find daily moments of spiritual rest, even when that runs counter to the patterns of the culture. We must find the balance between idolatry and idleness and seek to promote workplace flexibility.

Work-life balance matters. Work-life balance can save your health. It can help save your relationships with family and friends. It can help solve the mismatch you may be feeling between the needs of your family and the structure of your work. It can help you draw closer to God.

A colleague of mine at church tells a story that sums up why this issue matters to me, and why I believe it should matter for congregational leaders and all who seek healthy and happy lives:

A man came home from work one day, glad to be home but as tired as usual. He just wanted to rest and read the paper for a minute or two before tackling the home front and listening to his kids chatter. Just as he opened the door, his six-year-old son came up to him and asked, "Dad, how much do you make an hour?"

The father snapped, "Son, leave me alone with that kind of stuff, now. I'm tired. Go play, and we'll talk about this later."

The boy persisted, "Dad, just tell me, how much do you make an hour?"

The father said, "Why do you need to know that? Just go play and let me rest and read the paper. You know I'm always tired when I get home from work."

The boy kept going, "Please, Dad, just tell me how much you make an hour."

The father snapped again, "Twenty dollars. Now can I read the paper?"

The boy lit up and asked, "Can I borrow ten dollars from you?"

His father thundered, "Of course not. Now leave me alone for a while, Son."

After he read part of the paper and felt more rested and relaxed, the man started feeling guilty. He found his son in the backyard, just sitting on the swing and looking pensive. The father sat in the other swing and said, "Sorry I snapped at you, Son. Here is the ten dollars you wanted."

The boy lit up again. He reached in his pocket and pulled out a very crumbled ten-dollar bill, then said, "Now I have enough money. Dad, could I buy an hour of your time?"

Whenever I hear a story like that I am motivated—motivated to try to live a balanced life, motivated to try to be healthy, balanced, flexible, spiritual, and fully alive, for God's sake and for the sake of those people I love. May it be so for you and for me.

For Reflection

1. What is your work-life balance action plan?
2. What changes are you going to make in your life to achieve and maintain more balance? What ideas will you share with others?

Helpful Aids

APPENDIX 1

Time Reflection Chart

Use this and copies of this chart to detail each significant moment
of your day. Fill in the activity, beginning and ending time, and any
reflection on the activity. Take a day and map out how you spend
your time. The results may surprise you.

Name: _____

Date: _____

Page Number for Day: _____

_____ _____ _____ _____
Activity   Begin End   Reflection

_____ _____ _____ _____
Activity   Begin End   Reflection

_____ _____ _____ _____
Activity   Begin End   Reflection

_____ _____ _____ _____

Activity   Begin End   Reflection

_____ _____ _____ _____

Activity   Begin End   Reflection

_____ _____ _____ _____

Activity   Begin End   Reflection

_____ _____ _____ _____

Activity   Begin End   Reflection

_____ _____ _____ _____

Activity   Begin End   Reflection

General Reflections

_____

_____

_____

Tell Yourself about Your Time

Name: _____ Date: _____

1. I take a Sabbath day off each week.

    ___ yes   ___ no   ___ depends on the week

2. I observe a Sabbath on

    _____ Sunday   _____ another day   _____ no day

3. I observe some Sabbath rest every day.

    _____ yes   _____ no

4. I take vacation time each year that adds up to

    _____ 5 or more weeks   _____ 3-4 weeks

    _____ 0-2 weeks   _____ none

5. I take sick days each year.

    _____ yes   _____ no

    —— If yes, how many? _____

6. I feel I spend enough time with my family.

_____ yes   _____ no

If yes, how many hours each day? _____

7. I pray every day.

_____ yes _____ no

If yes, how many times each day? ___

8. I read Scripture each day.

_____ yes   _____ no

9. Each day I
   _____ write in a journal
   _____ exercise
   _____ meditate
   _____ relax

10. I spend time with friends each day.

_____ yes _____ no

11. I know and respect my limitations.

_____ yes _____ no

APPENDIX 3

Act and Evaluate Your Time

Name: _____ Date: _____

I. Over the next week, put into action some of the ideas in this book.

1. For five consecutive days, try to set aside time for Scripture reading each morning, prayer at noon, exercise or reading in the afternoon, and self-reflection and journaling in the evening.

2. Start your day meditating on the Word of God. There are many appropriate verses, especially the Psalms, but you might start with Psalm 23; Psalm 42:1-2; Ecclesiastes 3:1-8; Luke 10:38-42; Matthew 6:9-13; or Matthew 6:25-34.

3. In your prayer time, try to open yourself to the Holy Spirit through silence.

4. In your evening reflections, write out your thoughts about how you are spending your time, about your spiritual practices, about your balance in life, about the priorities you want to follow, about what limits you are trying to set for your life, about what you would like to eliminate, and about what changes you need to make in order to be more spiritually balanced and to steward better the gifts God has given you.

5. In all cases, try to be open to the indwelling of Christ.

6. After five days, reflect on how you have felt doing the spiritual practices. Do you feel like continuing these practices naturally, or are you glad you are finished?

II. Evaluate the impact of these practices on your spiritual journey.

1. I was able to continue my spiritual practices all five days.

___ yes   ___ no   ___ number of days completed

2. My life is more balanced as a result.

___ yes   ___ no

3. Scripture reading helps center me to begin my day.

___ yes   ___ no

4. Mid-day prayer helps me relax during the day.

___ yes   ___ no

5. Reflecting at the end of the day helps me set priorities.

___ yes   ___ no

6. Reflecting at the end of the day helps me feel grateful.

___ yes   ___ no

7. I will make changes to my daily activities to include more spiritual rest and balance.

___ yes   ___ no

8. I will now include daily Sabbath in my life.

___ yes   ___ no

9. I will continue to seek to open my life to God's holiness.

___ yes   ___ no

10. I believe spiritual practices and the example of Jesus can help me find more balance in life.

___ yes   ___ no

Turning Ideas into Actions

This appendix summarizes the main ideas, attitudes, and actions contained in this book. By seeing how they connect to and build on one another, they help us realize how the values of our faith can shape our beliefs and habits.

Ideas/Values	Attitudes/Beliefs	Actions/Habits
Stewardship	Saying no	Control of technology
Sanctification	Resting	Daily Sabbath
Self-care	Rethinking balance	Specific practices
Sabbath	Being intentional about time	Daily schedule

Notes

Preface
1. PCUSA Office of the General Assembly report, June 29, 2010.

Chapter 1: It's Personal
1. http://www.worklifebalance.com/worklifebalancedefined.html.
2. "Female Power," *The Economist*, December 30, 2009.
3. President Barack Obama, Speech to White House Forum on Workplace Flexibility, March 31, 2010.
4. Ellen Galinsky, Kerstin Aumann, and James T. Bond, *Times are Changing: Gender and Generation at Work and at Home* (Families and Work Institute, Revised August 2011).
5. Ibid.
6. Ibid.
7. Ruth Davis Konigsberg, "Chore Wars," *Time*, August 8, 2011, 45.
8. Tara Parker-Pope, "Now, Dad Feels as Stressed as Mom," *New York Times*, June 18, 2010.
9. Brad Harrington, Fred Van Deusen, and Jamie Ladge, *The New Dad: Exploring Fatherhood within a Career Context* (Boston: Boston College Center for Work & Family, 2010), 21.
10. Ibid.
11. Karen Kornbluh, "Families Valued," *Democracy: A Journal of Ideas*, Fall 2006, http://wwsw.democracyjournal.org/article.php?ID=6484.

Chapter 2: It's National

1. *Lord of the Rings: The Fellowship of the Ring* (New Line Cinema, 2001).
2. Chiung-Ya Tang and Shelley MacDermid Wadsworth, *Time and Workplace Flexibility, 2008 National Study of the Changing Workforce* (New York: Families and Work Institute, 2008), 11.
3. Suzanne M. Bianchi and Vanessa R. Wight, "The Long Reach of the Job: Employment and Time for Family Life," *Workplace Flexibility,* ed. Kathleen Christensen and Barbara Schneider (Ithaca: Cornell University Press, 2010); Christensen presentation at the New America Foundation, May 13, 2010.
4. Ibid.
5. Ibid.
6. Ibid.
7. Ibid.
8. Suzanne Bianchi, "Family Change and Time Allocation in American Families," paper for the "Focus on Workplace Flexibility" conference, November 2010, Table 1, p. 6; Steven Greenhouse, "Delayed Child Rearing, More Stressful Lives," *New York Times,* December 1, 2010.
9. Ibid.
10. John Rossheim, "Longer Work Hours Stress Families," Monster. com's 2004 Work/Life Balance survey, December 15, 2006.
11. Ellen Galinsky, James T. Bond, Stacy S. Kim, Lois Backon, Erin Brownfield, and Kelly Sakai, *Overwork in America: When the Way We Work Becomes Too Much* (New York: Families and Work Institute, 2005).
12. The Marlin Company, *The Tenth Annual "Attitudes in the American Workplace" Survey* (New Haven, CT, 2004).
13. Jennifer Hudson, "Workload and Sustained Stress Have Employees 'Just Getting By' During Workday," ComPsych Corporation, 2005.
14. Jeremy Reynolds, "In the Face of Conflict: Work-Life Conflict and Desired Work Hour Adjustments," *Journal of Marriage and Family* 67, no. 5 (2005): 1313-1331.
15. Kate Lorenz, "Five Warning Signs of Job Burnout," http://www. cnn.com/2006/US/Careers/03/15/cb.burnout/index.html.
16. Kathleen Christensen, presentation at the New America Foundation, May 13, 2010; Kerstin Aumann, Ellen Galinsky, Kelly Sakai, Melissa Brown, and James T. Bond, *The Elder Care Study:*

Everyday Realities and Wishes for Change, (New York: Families and Work Institute, 2010).

17. CCH, "Costly Problem of Unscheduled Absenteeism Continues to Perplex Employers," CCH Topic Spotlight, 2005, http://hr.cch.com/press/releases/absenteeism/default.asp.

18. Ibid.

19. Ibid.

20. Siri Agrell, "Stress: Public Health Enemy No. 1," *Globe and Mail*, December 8, 2010.

21. Institution of Occupational Safety and Health poll, January 10, 2011.

22. Sarah Thomas, "Family Friendly Firms Have More Productive Workers," *Boston Globe.* July 1, 2010; BrightHorizons/Northeastern University study.

23. Ibid.

24. White House Council of Economic Advisors, "Work-Life Balance and the Economics of Workplace Flexibility," March 2010.

25. Shira Offera and Barbara Schneider, "Revisiting the Gender Gap in Time-Use Patterns: Multitasking and Well-Being among Mothers and Fathers in Dual-Earner Families," *American Sociological Review*, 2011.

26. Ellen Galinsky, *Ask the Children: What America's Children Really Think about Working Parents* (New York: William Morrow, 1999).

27. Kathleen Christensen, presentation at the New America Foundation. May 13, 2010; Shira Offer and Barbara Schneider, "Multitasking Among Working Families: A Strategy for Dealing with the Time Squeeze," *Workplace Flexibility*, ed. Kathleen Christensen and Barbara Schneider, (Ithaca: Cornell University Press, 2010).

28. Ellen Galinsky, *Ask the Children.*

29. James T. Bond, Cynthia Thompson, Ellen Galinsky, and David Prottas, *Highlights of the National Study of the Changing Workforce: Dual Earner Couples* (New York: Families and Work Institute, 2002).

30. Suzanne Bianchi, "Family Change and Time Allocation in American Families," paper for the "Focus on Workplace Flexibility" conference, November 2010; Steven Greenhouse, "Delayed Child Rearing, More Stressful Lives," *New York Times,* December 1, 2010.

31. See Jennifer L. Matjasko and Amy F. Feldman, "Emotional Transmission Between Parents and Adolescents: The Importance of Work Characteristics and Relationship Quality," in *Being Together, Working Apart*, ed. Barbara Schneider and Linda J. Waite (Cambridge: Cambridge University Press, 2005), 138–58.

32. Mary Forgione, *Los Angeles Times*, November 11, 2010; American Psychological Association,"Stress in America," 2010.

33. I am indebted to my colleague at the New America Foundation, Kelleen Kaye, who conducted terrific research on this subject for our related paper, Kelleen Kaye and David Gray, "The Stress of Balancing Work and Family: The Impact on Parent and Child Health and the Need for Workplace Flexibility," New America Foundation, October 2007.

34. Tammy D. Allen and Jeremy Armstrong, "Further Examination of the Link Between Work-Family Conflict and Physical Health," *American Behavioral Scientist* 49, no. 9 (2006): 1204–22.

35. Christensen, presentation at the New America Foundation, May 13, 2010.

36. C. L. Ogden, M. D. Carroll, L. R. Curtin, M. M. Lamb, and K. M. Flegal, "Prevalence of High Body Mass Index in US Children and Adolescents, 2007–2008," *JAMA* 2010, 303(3): 242–9; Child Trends DataBank, 2006, based on data from the National Center for Health Statistics, available online at Childtrends.org.

37. Foundation for Child Development, 2007 Child Well-Being Index.

38. Jody Heymann, *The Widening Gap: Why America's Working Families are in Jeopardy and What Can Be Done About It* (New York: Basic Books, 2000).

39. Margaret S. Hart and Michelle L. Kelley, "Fathers' and Mothers' Work and Family Issues as Related to Internalizing and Externalizing Behavior of Children Attending Day Care," *Journal of Family Issues* 27, no. 2 (2006): 252–70; Elizabeth A. Vandewater and Jennifer E. Lansford, "A Family Process Model of Behaviors in Adolescents," *Journal of Marriage and Family* 67 (February 2005): 100–109.

40. Michael R. Frone, "Work-Family Conflict and Employee Psychiatric Disorders: The National Comorbidity Survey," *Journal of Applied Psychology* 85, no. 6 (2000).

41. Michael R. Frone, "Work-Family Conflict and Employee Psychiatric Disorders: The National Comorbidity Survey," *Journal of Applied Psychology* 85, no. 6 (2000).

42. Ibid., Hudson, "Workload and Sustained Stress."
43. Samuel Mann, "Job Stress and Blood Pressure: A Critical Appraisal of Reported Studies," *Current Hypertension Review* 2, no. 2. (2006): 127–38.
44. Agrell, "Stress: Public Health Enemy No. 1."
45. Lawrence Mishel, Jared Bernstein, and Heidi Shierholz, *The State of Working America 2008-2009* (Ithaca, NY: Cornell University Press, 2009).
46. Janet C. Gornick and Marcia K. Meyers, *Families That Work: Policies for Reconciling Parenthood and Employment* (New York: Russell Sage Foundation, 2005), 79–80.
47. International Labor Organization statistics, cited by G. E. Miller, "The U.S. is the Most Overworked Developed Nation in the World— When Do We Draw the Line?" International Labor Organization statistics, October 12, 2010, http://20somethingfinance.com/american-hours-worked-productivity-vacation/.
48. Dalton Conley, "Rich Man's Burden," *New York Times,* September 2, 2008, A23.
49. Ibid.
50. Ian Price, "Four-day Working Week? Three Cheers," *The Guardian,* April 15, 2011.
51. Ibid.
52. Ibid.
53. Ibid.
54. Bianchi and Wight, "The Long Reach of the Job."
55. Christensen, presentation at the New America Foundation, May 13, 2010.
56. Maria Shriver with Heather Boushey and Ann O'Leary, *The Shriver Report: A Woman's Nation Changes Everything,* ed Heather Boushey and Ann O'Leary (Washington, DC: Center for American Progress, 2009).
57. Steven Greenhouse, "Delayed Child Rearing, More Stressful Lives," *New York Times,* December 1, 2010.
58. Bianchi and Wight, "The Long Reach of the Job"; Christensen, presentation at the New America Foundation, May 13, 2010.
59. Christensen, presentation at the New America Foundation, May 13, 2010.

Chapter 3: It's Religious

1. David Van Biema, "Ten Forces Shaping the World," *Time*, March 12, 2009.
2. David W. Hall, *The Legacy of John Calvin: His Influence on the Modern World* (Phillipsburg, NJ: P & R Publishing, 2008).
3. John Calvin, "Commentary on Hosea: The Epistle Dedicatory," in William F. Keesecker, *A Calvin Reader* (Philadelphia: Westminster Press, 1985), 14.
4. John Calvin, "Commentary on I Timothy 6:6-9," in Keesecker, *Calvin Reader*, 128.
5. Puritan Reformers were Protestants who did not believe the Reformation had gone far enough in England. Some were Presbyterian, but they represented many denominations. Many of them came to America in order to have more control over their religious lives.
6. Max Weber, *The Protestant Ethic and the Spirit of Capitalism* (New York: Penguin Books, 1905), 2002 edition, 1; Peter Baehr and Gordon C. Wells, Introduction to Max Weber, *The Protestant Ethic and the Spirit of Capitalism* (London: Penguin Books, 2002), 5.
7. Weber, 131.
8. William Barclay, *The Letters to the Philippians, Colossians and Thessalonians* (Louisville, KY: Westminster Press, 1975), 217.
9. Ibid.
10. Ibid., xvi.
11. Weber, *Protestant Ethic*, 107–108.
12. Meister Eckhart in Karen J. Campbell, *German Mystical Writings: Hildegard of Bingen, Meister Eckhart, Jacob Boehme and Others* (London: Continuum International Publishing Group, 1991).
13. John Calvin, *Institutes of the Christian Religion*, 3.10.6 in *Calvin's Institutes*, ed. Donald K. McKim (Louisville, KY: Westminster John Knox, 2001), 92.
14. Hall, *Legacy of John Calvin*, 27.
15. Ibid.
16. Ibid., 28.
17. Donald K. McKim, *Presbyterian Beliefs* (Louisville, KY: Geneva Press, 2003), 72.
18. Calvin, *Institutes*, 3.21.5.
19. Weber, *Protestant Ethic*, xviii.

20. McKim, *Calvin's Institutes,* 73.
21. Weber, *Protestant Ethic,* 76.
22. Ibid.
23. Ibid., xx.
24. Ibid., xxxix.
25. Ibid., xvii.
26. Ibid.
27. Ibid., 75.
28. Matthew Henry, *The Worth of the Soul, Works of the Puritan Divines,* cited in Weber, *Protestant Ethic,* 178.
29. Richard Baxter, *Christian Directory,* cited in Weber, *Protestant Ethic,* 177.
30. Richard Baxter, *Christian Directory,* 1673; Richard Baxter, *The Practical Works of Richard Baxter: An Essay on His Genius, Works, and Times; And a Portrait,* Soli Deo Gloria Publishers, Four volume edition, September 1997, 468; Weber, *Protestant Ethic,* 178.
31. Richard Baxter, in Scott A. Appelrouth and Laura D. Edles, *Classical and Contemporary Sociological Theory: Text and Readings,* ed. Scott A. Appelrouth and Laura D. Edles (Newbury Park, CA: Pine Forge Press, 2011), 176.
32. Baxter, cited in Weber, *Protestant Ethic,* 106–107.
33. Baxter might have appreciated this modern joke: "A church school lesson one Sunday was about the second commandment, 'You shall not make for yourself an idol.' The teacher questioned the children, 'Are there any idols in America?' 'Yes,' replied one boy, 'my mother says my father is unbelievably idle.'"
34. Weber, *Protestant Ethic,* 107.
35. Everett H. Emerson, *John Cotton* (New Haven, CT: College & University Press, 1965), 45.
36. Perry Miller, ed., *The American Puritans: Their Prose and Poetry* (New York: Anchor Books, 1956), 173.
37. Mike McMullen, "Attracting and Keeping Congregational Members," Faith Communities Today, 2008, http://faithcommunitiestoday.org/sites/faithcommunitiestoday.org/files/Attracting%20and%20Keeping%20Members.pdf.
38. Scott McConnell, "How Protestant Pastors Spend Their Time," Lifeway Research, 2008.
39. Rick Warren, "Are You Spending Too Much Time in Meetings," *Rick Warren's Ministry Toolbox,* www.pastors.com.

40. "2010 Compensation and Personnel Policies for Pastors and Certified Christian Educators," National Capital Presbytery, Rockville, MD.

41. Paul Vitello, "Taking a Break from the Lord's Work," *New York Times*, August 1, 2010.

42. Ibid.

43. Ibid.

44. Ibid.; Gwen Wagstrom Halaas, *The Right Road: Life Choices for Clergy* (Minneapolis, MN: Augsburg Fortress, 2004).

45. Vitello, "Taking a Break."

46. Ibid.

47. Ibid.

48. Ibid.

49. Kimberly Morgan and Sally Steenland, "The Challenge of Faith," in Shriver, *The Shriver Report*, 255–56.

Chapter 4: We Need to Change Our Thinking

1. E. A. Livingstone, *The Concise Oxford Dictionary of the Christian Church* (Oxford: Oxford University Press, 1977), 4.

2. "The Life and Times of John Calvin," ChristianityToday.com, October 1, 1986.

3. http://www.merriam-webster.com/dictionary/stewardship.

4. Calvin, *Institutes*, 3.7.5.

5. Stanton adds: "*Halacha* in the Jewish tradition is codified in the *Mishneh* and elaborated upon through the rabbinic discussions and debates of the *Gemara*. Together, these books comprise the Talmud—one version of which relies upon Palestinian rabbinic commentary, the other of which relies upon Babylonian rabbinic commentary."

6. Joshua Stanton, commissioned paper (unpublished) for the New America Foundation, May 2010.

7. Calvin, *Institutes*, 3.7.5.

8. Calvin, "Commentary on Hebrews 13:15," in Keesecker, *Calvin Reader*, 25.

9. Bruce Douglass, lecture at Reformed Institute retreat, Meadowkirk Conference Center, March 21, 2007.

10. In the Reformed tradition, Puritan John Cotton provides helpful guidance on finding one's calling. Cotton describes the conditions of a "warrantable calling" in his essay "Christian Calling" which

includes: God must give the person gifts for the particular calling; The person must have the intellect and emotional strength to succeed at the vocation; A calling that serves God cannot just be self-interest, it has to serve the greater good; One should practice one's calling in community; One should look for signs of God's providence in one's life and follow where God is leading; One must have an attitude of humility in one's work, relying on God's grace and blessings; One should work cheerfully, humbly with an eye towards Heaven; In all, one should choose a vocation for which one is suited and that furthers the common good; It's not a question of doing what one wants, but knowing, discovering one's place. [Everett H. Emerson, *John Cotton* (New Haven, CT: College and University Press, 1965), 45.]

11. Calvin, *Institutes,* 3.10.6.
12. William J. Bouwsma, *John Calvin: A Sixteenth Century Portrait,* (Oxford: Oxford University Press, 1988), 186.
13. Rick Warren, "Are you spending too much time in meetings?" *Rick Warren Ministry Toolbox,* www.pastors.com.
14. Ibid.
15. Henry David Thoreau quoted by Tal Ben Shahar, *Happier* (New York: McGraw Hill, 2007), 45.
16. Joshua Stanton, paper for the New America Foundation, May 2010.
17. Calvin, *Institutes,* 3.1.2.
18. John Calvin, "Sermon on Deut. 5:12-14, June 1555" in Richard Gaffin, *Calvin and the Sabbath: The Controversy of Applying the Fourth Commandment* (Scotland: Mentor, 1998; reprinted 2009), 109.
19. John Calvin, "Commentary on Genesis 50:15," in Keesecker, *Calvin Reader,* 122.
20. Tim Kasser quoted by Shahar, *Happier,* 154; Tim Kasser, "Time Affluence as a Path Towards Personal Happiness and Ethical Business Practices: Empirical Evidence from Four Studies." Co-authored with K.M. Sheldon, *Journal of Business Ethics* 84 (2009), 243–55.
21. Ibid.
22. Gershon Brin, *The Concept of Time in the Bible and the Dead Sea Scrolls* (Boston: Brill Academic Publishers, 2001), 1; James Barr, *Biblical Words for Time,* (Naperville, IL: Alec R. Allenson, Inc., 1962), 24.

23. James L. Crenshaw, *Ecclesiastes* (Philadelphia: Westminster Press, 1987), 92.

24. Niels-Erik Andreasen, *The Christian Use of Time* (Nashville: Abingdon Press, 1978), 14.

25. For more insights into the practice of Sabbath and its connection to holy, God-filled time, see Judith Shulevitz's compelling book, *The Sabbath World: Glimpses of a Different Order of Time* (New York: Random House, 2010).

26. Niels-Erik, *The Christian Use of Time*, 3.

27. Lewis Carroll, *Alice's Adventures in Wonderland and Through the Looking-Glass*, originally published in 1865 (Las Vegas, NV: Cosimo, Inc., 2010), 42.

Chapter 5: We Need to Change Our Habits

1. Tal Ben Shahar, *Happier* (New York: McGraw Hill, 2007), 9.

2. Stacy Johnson, "Things Babies Born in 2011 Will Never Know," *Money Talks News,* January 5, 2011. http://finance.yahoo.com/family-home/article/111745/things-babies-born-in-2011-will-never-know?mod=family-kids_parents.

3. Deloitte LLP, *Trust in the Workplace: 2010 Ethics and Workplace Survey,* July 26, 2010. http://www.deloitte.com/assets/Dcom-UnitedStates/Local%20Assets/Documents/us_2010_Ethics_and_Workplace_Survey_report_071910.pdf.

4. Barbara Schneider, remarks at "Promoting Children's Wellbeing: The Role of Workplace Flexibility" event, Workplace Flexibility 2010 and New America Foundation, Hart Senate Office Building, Washington, DC, September 26, 2006.

5. Ibid.

6. Ibid.

7. Nancy Trejos, "Unplugging Right Along," *The Washington Post,* February 6, 2011.

8. William Powers, *Hamlet's Blackberry: A Practical Philosophy for Building a Good Life in the Digital Age* (New York: HarperCollins, 2010), 5.

9. Ibid., 83–84.

10. Ibid., 185.

11. Study by the International Center for Media & the Public Agenda (ICMPA) at the University of Maryland, April 21, 2010. http://theworldunplugged.wordpress.com/.

12. Donna St. George, "On Family Beach Vacations, Text-loving Teens Stay Plugged In," *The Washington Post,* July 4, 2010.
13. Trejos, "Unplugging Right Along."
14. Ibid.
15. Calvin, *Institutes,* 2.8.32.
16. Greg Tobin, *Holy Holidays! The Catholic Origins of Celebration* (New York: Palgrave MacMillian, 2011), 135.
17. Elsie Anne McKee, ed., *John Calvin: Writings on Pastoral Piety* (Mahwah, NJ: Paulist Press, 2001), 253; Richard Gaffin, *Calvin and the Sabbath* (Scotland: Christian Focus Publications, 2000), 114.
18. Calvin, *Institutes,* 2.8.30.
19. Ibid.
20. Gaffin, *Calvin and the Sabbath,* 36.
21. Ibid., 108.
22. John Bate, *Cyclopedia of Illustrations of Moral and Religious Truths* (London: Elliot Stock, 1865).
23. *Evan Almighty* (Universal Pictures, 2007).
24. Ibid.
25. Vicki Robin, Joe Dominguez, and Monique Tilford, *Your Money or Your Life: Transforming Your Relationship with Money and Achieving Financial Independence* (New York: Viking Penguin, 1992).
26. http://rowdykittens.com/2011/09/quotes/.
27. Scott Mayerowitz. "Americans Afraid to Take Full Vacations." ABC News Travel quoting an IPSOS/Reuters Survey, August 10, 2010. For more information on the health benefits of taking vacations, see Kim Painter, "Why Time Off Is Well Spent," *USATODAY,* July 14, 2008, 6D.
28. http://creatingminds.org/quotes/habit.htm.
29. Lewis Bayly, *The Practice of Piety,* 1994 ed. (London: Soli Deo Gloria Ministries, Publisher, 1611), 1.
30. Calvin, "Commentary on Daniel 6:10," in Keesecker, *Calvin Reader,* 23.
31. David Robinson, *The Busy Family's Guide to Spirituality* (New York: Crossroad Publishing, 2000), 95, 147.

Chapter 6: We Need to Change Our Societal Structures

1. http://www.theglobeandmail.com/news/national/time-to-lead/work-life-balance/work-life-balance-best-of-the-series/article1824260/.

2. Stephen M. Wing, "Work-Life Balance," cited in Yvonne Siu, Corporate Voices for Working Families blog, December 5, 2010. http://corporatevoices.wordpress.com/2010/12/05/corporate-voices-contributes-foreword-to-work-life-balance-special-report/.
3. WorldatWork, "Survey on Workplace Flexibility," February 14, 2011.
4. Yvonne Siu, "Focus on Workplace Flexibility," Corporate Voices for Working Families blog, December 7, 2010.
5. Workplace Flexibility 2010 policy platform. WF2010 has given permission for the inclusion of this platform. http://workplaceflexibility2010.org/index.php/policy_components/.
6. Ibid.
7. Ibid.
8. Ibid.
9. The briefing included speakers from the Shalem Institute for Spiritual Formation, Georgetown University, and *Islamic* magazine and was cosponsored by Representatives Mark Souder (R-IN) and Emanuel Cleaver (D-MO).
10. The federal Office of Personnel Management has made a Results Oriented Work Environment a priority for the federal government.
11. These suggestions are influenced by my collaboration over the years with Workplace Flexibility 2010. Information on additional ideas can be found in the WF2010 platform on flexible work arrangements. http://workplaceflexibility2010.org/images/uploads/reports/report_1.pdf; http://workplaceflexibility2010.org/index.php/policy_components/.
12. Kathryn Fonner, University of Wisconsin-Milwaukee, *Journal of Applied Communication Research*, November 2010, cited in Federal Daily Staff, "Teleworkers Experience Lower Amount of Stress, Study Finds," December 1, 2010. http://fcw.com/articles/2010/11/30/teleworkers-experience-lower-amounts-of-stress-study-finds.aspx.